Tricks of the Trade

101 Psychological Techniques to Help Children Grow and Change

By Lawrence E. Shapiro, Ph.D.

Childswork/Childsplay
Plainview, New York

Tricks of the Trade
101 Psychological Tricks to Help Children Grow and Change

By Lawrence E. Shapiro, Ph.D.
Design by Christopher Laughlin

Childswork/Childsplay publishes products for mental health professionals, teachers and parents who wish to help children with their developmental, social and emotional growth. For questions, comments, or to request a free catalog describing hundreds of games, toys, books, and other counseling tools, call 1-800-962-1141 or visit our Web site at www.childswork.com

© 1994 Childswork/Childsplay, LLC
A Guidance Channel Company
135 Dupont Street
Plainview, NY 11803
1-800-962-1141
www.childswork.com

ISBN 1-882732-20-0

Other books by Lawrence E. Shapiro, Ph.D.

- *A.D.D Tool Kit*

- *All Feelings Are OK: It's What You Do with Them That Counts*

- *Anger Control Tool Kit*

- *Every Time I Blow My Top I Lose My Head*

- *Face Your Feelings!*

- *Forms for Helping the ADHD Child*

- *Forms for Use in Counseling Children*

- *How I Learned To Be Considerate of Others*

- *In Control: A Book of Games To Teach Children Self-Control Skills*

- *Jumpin' Jake Settles Down: A Workbook to Help Impulsive Children Learn to Think Before They Act*

- *Short-Term Therapy with Children*

- *Sometimes I Drive My Mom Crazy, But I Know She's Crazy About Me: A Self-Esteem Book for ADHD Children*

- *Sometimes I Like To Fight, But I Don't Do It Much Anymore*

- *The Building Blocks of Self-Esteem: A Skill-Oriented Approach to Teaching Self-Worth*

- *The Very Angry Day That Amy Didn't Have*

TABLE OF CONTENTS

Motivating and Engaging Children in the Therapeutic Process

Techniques to Enhance Communication

Diagnostic Techniques

Cognitive Techniques

Teaching and Enhancing Social Skills

Parenting Techniques

Building a Strong Self-Concept

Play Techniques

Dedication

I dedicate this book to my father, Theodore Shapiro, who in an odd way was my inspiration for this book. Actually, my father didn't like psychologists, and he seemed mildly disappointed when I chose the profession. He was a wholesale meat distributor, a "meat man," as he used to say, as opposed to a "poultry man," whom he also didn't think much of. But his job was just his job. Pranks and jokes were his avocation.

Every day offered an opportunity to pull some strange prank or another. He served rubber chickens at family dinners. He put live crabs in the toilet bowl at work. Two decades before the mobile phone was invented, he tied the cord of a phone receiver to his belt and stood in front of his store pretending to hear a phone ringing. Then he would go up to a complete stranger and tell him that the phone was for him. I watched him do this dozens of times, and each time the stranger talked into the phone expecting an answer, even though he could clearly see that this was just a receiver tied to my father's belt.

It was my father's ability to redefine reality that so impressed me. For two years, when my father was about the age that I am now, he drove his old Ford station wagon as if it was a horse. I find it hard to explain to people now, but he literally tied two ropes to his steering wheel, which he treated as reins, and talked to his car as if it were a horse. My father wasn't delusional; he recognized that this was funny, and yet to ride with him in the car you would never have guessed that he was doing anything but riding his horse to work.

Frequently, people ask me how I come up with my creative ideas. I shrug and say, "I don't know." But I do know. Whether it is through genetics or observation, I am my father's son. Granted, my ideas are a little more focused and problem-oriented, but I believe that they spring from the same well of imagination and zest for living. I hope so. My father's "tricks" were for his special trade, which was living exuberantly. I hope I do as well.

Introduction

The Magic of Psychotherapy with Children

At one time or another, everyone who works with troubled children has the fantasy of waving a magic wand and making things better. With one grand gesture, all the problems would go away. We all believe in our hearts that children shouldn't suffer, and it is only natural to wish their problems would disappear.

Those who work with children retain some of the fantasies of childhood:

- That there really is magic.

- That there really are genies or fairies or angels who grant wishes.

- That wanting something really badly can make it happen.

But as mental health professionals, we are exposed on a daily basis to the harshest of realities. Life isn't fair. Children are vulnerable. Even our best intentions and most brilliant interventions don't always help.

This juxtaposition between our childlike need to want to magically help children and the daily presence of reality factors beyond our control can tire us, take the edge of enthusiasm from our work, and eventually burn us out.

But there are answers in the middle ground between our childlike fantasies and our adult demands for reality. Most therapists have these answers; expert therapists have many of them. I call them "tricks of the trade."

Tricks of the trade in child psychotherapy are the idiosyncratic interventions that keep children engaged in therapy, that promote growth towards a particular therapeutic goal, and that are, most of all, fun.

Did I say fun? No, that is too flat a word. The best tricks of the child psychotherapy trade are titillating, provocative, charming, surprising, endearing ... MAGICAL! The best techniques are not only effective for the child, but they trigger a very unique "curative" force in the therapist. They make therapists come alive. They make us enjoy the task of psychotherapy, which might otherwise range from the mundane to the heart-rending. Every therapist who works with children has a different kind of magic that he or she practices and, therefore, different tricks.

There are behaviorists and cognitively-oriented therapists whose magic is in the science of psychology. There are artistic therapists who use music or art or dance to create their particular brand of magic. There are clownish therapists who use silliness as a way to engage children. There are rough-and-tumble therapists who get physically involved with their clients and may emphasize recreational therapy as a way to achieve their therapeutic goals. And there are storytelling therapists who have a particular literary gift and weave through their therapy a gentle rhythm of symbols and fables amid the true poetry of childhood.

Personally, I like fun stuff – gimmicks, gadgets, magic tricks, stupid and surprising toys. I'd like to do my therapy in Willy Wonka's Chocolate Factory or Pee-wee's Playhouse. I'd like to have trap doors and chairs that talk, slides that take you to a different floor, robots doing the cleaning ... you get the point. Unfortunately, that kind of stuff is rather expensive, so I've settled for simpler gimmicks, gadgets and contraptions and search for the unusual products that bring an element of surprise and delight to working with children.

The tricks of the trade that I have included in this book come from many types of therapists. As a publisher as well as a lecturer, I talk to creative therapists all around the country. When we talk, I find that my attention always picks up when I hear about a particular "trick." I find that I'm saying to myself, "That's clever. I'll have to remember that." In fact, those are exactly the things that I do remember.

I love to hear about these tricks and, if possible, I love to use them. I also like to think about why they work, and when I take the time to study them, I inevitably remember something new about childhood or the process of doing psychotherapy.

Looking at why these tricks work in therapy is like analyzing why a joke is funny. Understanding the mechanics of a joke doesn't make it any more or any less funny. A joke is funny both in its content and in its telling, and why it is funny doesn't really matter.

But it does matter if you are a comedian by trade. A comic is interested in the mechanics of the joke so that he can construct his own jokes based on what he has analyzed. Understanding how a joke is constructed makes it easier for the comic to tweak it just a little bit and make it that much funnier.

The tricks of psychotherapy in this book have an analogous relationship to the therapist as do jokes to the comic. They have been selected so that, for the most part, they can stand alone and can be implemented effectively by a therapist with only a minimum amount of experience. Some of the techniques are like really good jokes; they are so good and eloquently simple that anyone can use them and still get the expected results. Other techniques require a little practice and thought. Sometimes before we tell jokes, we think about them. Why are they funny? We rehearse them in our mind, and then we wait for just the right opportunity and audience to try them out. Some people are naturally funny and spontaneous, and they can make us laugh through their natural talent for wit and humor. So it is with some therapists, who have an innate ability to weave in the right technique at the right time in therapy.

As you skim through this book, you will note that the techniques cover a wide range of theoretical positions. Research has shown that most therapists, even those who say they subscribe to a single school of thought, draw their psychological techniques from a variety of schools of psychotherapy. And why not? Arnold Lazarus, the first author to write about using a systematic multimodal system of techniques, notes that while theories may be incompatible, techniques are not (*Multimodal Therapy*, Basic Books, 1980). Psychodynamically oriented therapists will occasionally use a behavioral intervention, client-centered therapists will use a more direct approach, and family therapists will decide to see a child in individual therapy. Therapists, particularly child therapists, are much less tied to a specific school of thought than they are eager to do whatever works.

This is not to say, however, that the techniques in this book, or any other set of techniques, are atheoretical or should be practiced out of context. Although I have primarily tried to select methods that require little specialized training (as opposed to techniques such as hypnotherapy, biofeedback, the sand tray technique, etc.), it is still important for the therapist to understand that even the simplest technique is based on specific principles and theories, and that those theories and principles must be understood for the technique to work effectively. Time and again I have seen good techniques fail (particularly basic techniques like the Token Economy System), not because they were the wrong technique, but because they were not applied consistently, respecting the theory and principles from which they were developed.

For this reason, I have tried to identify the theory or school of thought from which each technique was derived. It is assumed that, in using these techniques, the counselor or therapist will have at least a basic familiarity with the principles on which the theory is based and will adhere to them.

In writing this book, it was my intention to stimulate the creativity of child therapists and counselors to find and develop techniques that excite them and stimulate the "magical" aspects of their work. However, it is also worth noting some guidelines that should be considered in choosing and implementing techniques.

Respect the parameters of the therapeutic context.

Every therapist or counselor has certain boundaries that define the context in which they work. For most therapists working with adults, the boundaries are almost always the four walls of the therapy office. But working with children frequently makes these boundaries more intangible. Nearly all therapists who work with children spend a significant amount of time providing therapeutic advice by phone. School counselors, psychologists, social workers, and others find themselves making therapeutic interventions in hallways, classrooms, the playground...virtually anyplace they can grab a quiet moment. Other therapists may make home visits or may do therapy at the site where the problem exists (e.g., for school phobias or other specific fears).

Wherever the therapist is working, he or she must recognize that the boundaries of therapy must be respected, even though they may have become more intangible. The therapist is always a special person in a child's life, and that "specialness" must accompany him or her wherever therapy is practiced.

Never do something outside the office that someone else can do.

I believe that therapists can be effective in many settings, not just within the confines of an office. But I recognize that leaving the office has inherent risks and ethical considerations, and I use an important rule of thumb in determining whether it is really necessary for me to leave the safer confines of my office. That rule is simply: If someone else can do a particular task or technique, the therapist should let him or her do it.

For example, I frequently hear of therapists or counselors taking children outside the therapy room for ice cream, to buy a reward, or for other special treats. Unless this is in the context of "Milieu Therapy" (which it rarely is), I don't consider this an appropriate therapeutic intervention. This is a job that a parent or other person in the child's life should be doing; there is nothing inherently therapeutic about going out for a treat with a child.

There are also the therapists who play computer games with children as a reward. I have had several therapists tell me that children like this and that this strengthens the therapeutic alliance. But again, I am skeptical. I know children enjoy these activities, and there is something to that, but where is the magic? Anyone can play a computer game with a child, and since computer games are mostly parallel play activities, children will enjoy

4

them just as much when they play by themselves. Since most children have more than adequate opportunity to play computer games outside the therapy session, what really makes this technique special?

Weigh the intrusiveness vs. the power of the technique.

As I have stated elsewhere (*Short-Term Therapy with Children*, Childswork/Childsplay, LLC, 1994), therapists or counselors must always weigh the power or effectiveness of the technique against the degree to which it intrudes into, or disrupts, the child's life. In the vast majority of cases, the more power a particular technique has, the more it is disruptive to the child, his education, or his family. Like it or not, there is usually a direct relationship between the power of a particular therapeutic technique and its intrusiveness.

For example, we know that stimulant medication can be highly effective for more than 80% of children diagnosed with ADHD, when combined with other techniques. The medication is highly effective, but it is also intrusive. For obvious reasons, no one wants to see a child taking medication, and yet research has suggested that in most cases the perceived problems that are associated with medication are far outweighed by the benefits. This same consideration must be made with every intervention selected for a child: Is the intrusiveness of the technique justified by its potential benefits?

Motivating and Engaging Children in the Therapeutic Process

The diverse techniques in this section have one thing in common: They're fun. As therapists or counselors, we must be sympathetic to the natural reluctance of children to come to see us for help. In most cases, they are in our offices on someone else's demand. Perhaps they have acted badly. Perhaps they are suffering from great emotional turmoil. Whatever the reason, children will undoubtedly meet us with a mixture of apprehension, anxiety, and embarrassment. From the moment we meet children, we try to put them at ease, to establish a relationship built on trust and compassion. But with some children this is a formidable task. They may be belligerent, uncooperative, or simply uninterested in our offers of help.

The techniques in this section are designed to help in establishing therapeutic alliances with children and to motivate them towards therapeutic work. As is true throughout this book, the techniques you like best are the ones that are most likely to be effective for you.

#1. The Applause Box: A Reward That Children Can't Resist

Theory: *Behavior Therapy; Positive Reinforcement*

Most children are interested in tangible tokens which they can win through their improved behavior, like stickers or chips, which can then be used to "purchase" other rewards, like small toys or special privileges. Some children, however, are so used to getting things that they are not impressed by a therapist's treasures, and some thought must be given to motivating these children to change.

One trick that almost never fails to get the attention of young children is ... applause! For many years, I kept an Applause Box on my desk, to use as a reward for children who had done something special or achieved a required level of points on their behavioral charts. When the button on the Applause Box was pressed, it gave about 30 seconds of the most enthusiastic applause, to the delight and amazement of the child. It is difficult to explain the thrill in a child's eyes when he or she hears a crowd of people clapping and bellowing: "Bravo! You did it! Congratulations!" It is as if children are transported to some magical stage, where all the people they love most are giving them the attention and adulation they crave.

Unfortunately, the original Applause Box is no longer available. However, I can tell you how to make one yourself with just a few moments of your time. You will need a tape recorder and about five people. The people can be strangers to the child, but it is preferable if you have people who are important in the child's life (Mom, Dad, grandparents, older siblings, teachers, etc.). When the tape recorder is set up, just signal your group to applaud all at once, the louder the better. After about ten seconds of enthusiastic applause, ask three or four people to make specific comments directly into the microphone with the applause continuing in the background. For example:

Mom: "I'm so proud of you!"

Dad: "Bravo! Bravo! You've done it!"

Grandma: "Wonderful job! We love you!"

The tape recorder with your recorded applause can be presented to the child, in a decorated box with smiling faces, photographs, hands clapping, etc. When the child completes a required task or wins a required number of points, just open the box and turn on the recording. Watch what happens!

Warning: In almost every instance, the child will ask to hear the applause again and again, but remember, this is a reward that must be won. If a child won one sticker with his or her behavior, you wouldn't give him or her another one because he or she asked for it. This would go against the proven principles of providing positive reinforcement. The applause, like any other reward, must be withheld to keep its value. The child can only hear the applause as a reward for specific behavioral goals or achievements.

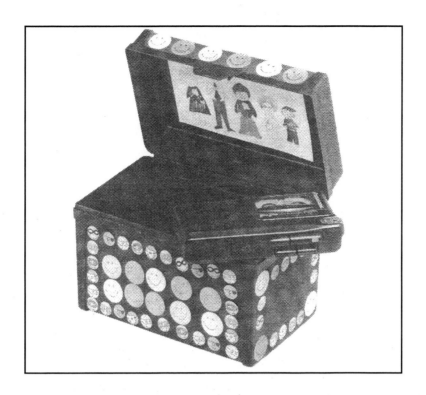

The Applause Box consists of three to five minutes of tape-recorded applause.
Use any tape recorder in a decorated box.

#2. Carnival Games as Rewards

Theory: *Positive Reinforcement; Token Economy*

Behavioral therapists know that one of the most important principles of getting people to change their behavior has to do with the strength of the reinforcer. If you want a child to control his or her temper, you probably wouldn't reward self-control with an extra serving of broccoli. Maybe you'd give him or her stickers, which he or she might like, but not love. Or maybe you would give him or her a cookie when he or she brought home a good report. Big deal. He or she probably gets cookies all the time.

To really effect behavioral change, the reward must be better than the "rewards" that the child gets by not changing the problem behavior. We often forget how hard it is to change a behavior, because even though the behavior may seem very self-defeating and dysfunctional, there are very real reasons that it came about and became entrenched in the child's life.

To help a child to change, you must follow the "salivating principle." A reward should be so good, so cool, so totally awesome, that the child should be drooling at the thought of getting it.

In today's materialistic society, this is not an easy task. Kids get a lot of stuff for doing very little. Since you are not going to spend $5,000 to get the child that motorized miniature Ferrari that he or she can actually ride in, you've got to make up in fun for what you lack in funds.

I find that nothing works quite like carnival tickets. Children don't know that the same tickets that you pay for dearly at a carnival or fun park can be purchased by the thousands for a few dollars at large stationery stores. When a child wins points by making progress towards some goal, I give a carnival ticket for each point. To a child, this is hard currency.

I then let the child cash the tickets in for simple "carnival" games that I set up in my office. For five tickets, he or she can play a simple basketball game, or knock down plastic milk bottles, or throw Velcro darts. I make the games really easy, and the prizes are more tickets! (For example, it costs five tickets to play "Knock the Bottles," but when you knock them all down with three balls, you get 10 tickets back!) Children can at any time cash in their tickets for carnival-type prizes that I keep on display (e.g., a little stuffed animal is 50 tickets, a magic trick is 100 tickets, etc.).

In using carnival tickets and letting children win more by playing games, I usually achieve the "salivating effect" that I am striving for. Immediate rewards, fun games, long-term rewards, a strong perceived value...all are good ingredients for motivating children to change.

#3. The Reward Store

Theory: *Behavior Therapy; Positive Reinforcement*

Many therapists develop a reward "menu" for children who are on a token economy program, presenting them with a hierarchy of rewards that can be won when they reach specific behavioral goals. However, young children, or children who are hard to motivate, may not be impressed with a written list of rewards, and may respond much more positively to tangible rewards.

Some schools with classes for emotionally/behaviorally handicapped children use a reward "store." Students have the opportunity to earn points or tokens throughout the day, and then at designated times during the week they can use the tokens to buy candy, small toys, pencils, or other inexpensive items. For some students, the idea of going to the Reward Store can be just as exciting and motivating as actually getting the reward.

A Reward Store can also be set up in a therapist's or counselor's office or in the home. All you need are four or five shoe boxes, each marked with a number depicting the point value for the contents of the box (e.g., 5 points, 10 points, 15 points and so on). In the 5-point box there could be stickers; in the 10-point box some small candy bars or trinkets; in a box with a higher point value there could be the picture of an activity that the child is saving up points for (e.g., a trip to the movies, the zoo, etc.). The contents of these boxes can be changed occasionally to provide renewed interest to the child or children on the behavioral program. It is usually best to limit the time that a child can select a reward to five minutes or less.

Carnival tickets are great immediate reinforcers.
Children think they are more valuable than gold!

Children can earn tickets, which they can use to play carnival-type games and then win prizes. This is a two-tiered type of reinforcement that kids love.

#4. Who's the Patient, Anyway? When the Therapist Takes on the Role as Patient

Theory: *Family Therapy; Psychodrama*

Dr. David Greenwald, an author and child and family therapist, has a flair for disarming clients and simultaneously engaging them. Dr. Greenwald has seen many latency-age boys who come to him for the first time, usually distrustful, sometimes sullen, nearly always wary. One way Dr. Greenwald puts these children at ease is by turning the tables of psychotherapy and switching the expected role of the therapist and patient.

"Ask me any three questions about myself," Dr. Greenwald begins, and he sits back, arms folded on his chest, ready to respond. The child, jolted by this role reversal, is typically both taken aback and intrigued. With this simple invitation, the child is given the power of being the therapist, even if just for a moment, and is receiving the therapeutic message, "'This is not a one-sided relationship. I will be vulnerable, just as I am asking you to be. I will trust you, if you will trust me!"

#5. Jokes and Riddles

Theory: *Developmental*

Dr. Richard A. Gardner has made an invaluable contribution to the field of child psychotherapy when he redefined the term "resistance" from the lexicon of psychoanalysis. Trained in psychoanalytic theory himself, Dr. Gardner had been taught that one of the basic tenets of psychotherapy, including child psychotherapy, was to break down the patient's resistance to bringing unconscious material into conscious awareness.

But this type of "insight," Dr. Gardner now notes, is largely irrelevant when working with children, because most child patients are not capable of what Jean Piaget calls formal reasoning or abstract thinking. Dr. Gardner defines "resistance" in child psychotherapy as anything that keeps the child from actively participating in the therapeutic process. Nearly 25 years after he wrote *Psychotherapeutic Approaches with the Resistant Child* (Jason Aronson,

1975), Gardner has proven himself the grand master of developing techniques to engage children in therapy.

Jokes and riddles are among his favorite ploys. Humor is such a basic part of the human condition that it is almost impossible to resist a good joke or even a bad one. Jokes and riddles lend themselves to an immediate connection between two people, a connection based on shared experience, giving and taking, and fun. Here are a few of Dr. Gardner's favorite riddles:

"Why don't hummingbirds sing?"

They don't know the words.

"What is Smokey the Bear's middle name?"

The.

"What is invisible and smells like worms?"

A bird's fart.

Many of Dr. Gardner's best jokes might be referred to as bathroom humor. But why not use the language and themes to which children relate? Jokes and humor are a way of relating to a child on a primary level, like making faces at an infant. When you get a child to smile and laugh with you, the relationship has begun.

Family Drawings
#6. Your Family Museum
#7. What Animals Would Your Family Be?
#8. Designing Your Family Store

Theory: *Family Therapy; Art Therapy*

Therapists typically think of projective drawing techniques as a one-on-one activity with a child, but drawing is a tool that can be used with a whole family as well. Therapeutice art activities can be done in a family session or sent home as family "homework." The concrete nature of any task makes it easier for families to complete that task successfully.

As the following examples illustrate, the drawing assignment can foster communication, problem-solving, defining a common goal, a sense of family identity, and so on. As art therapists know, this type of nonverbal activity can be very fruitful in terms of revealing both intrapsychic and interpersonal therapeutic data.

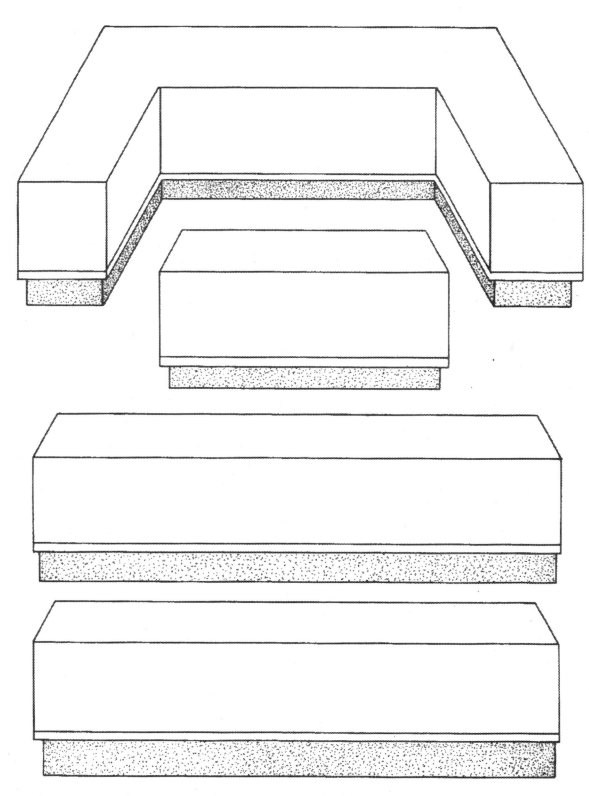

Suppose your family was so famous that you decided to make a whole museum about your life together. What are some of the most important things that would be exhibited?

Imagine a witch has turned your whole family into animals! What animal would each person be? How would they get along?

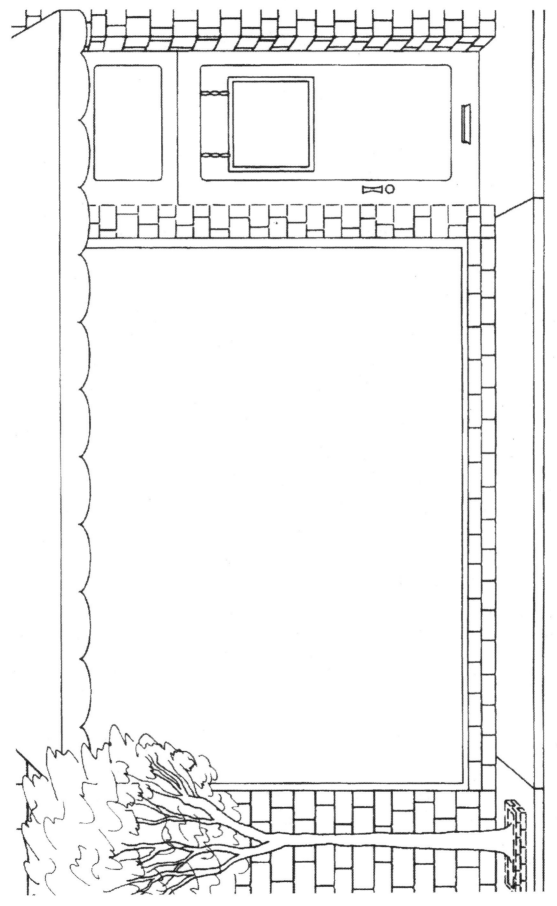

Pretend your whole family is opening a store. What will you sell? Design a window display that will make people want to come inside. Don't forget to name your store.

#9. A Psychological Scavenger Hunt

Theory: *Strategic Family Therapy*

Every therapist or counselor working with children will at some time need input from a child's family. There is a wide spectrum of techniques that can be used to obtain this information, from questionnaires to phone interviews, to formal meetings or treatment sessions with the family. Techniques will be chosen based on the cooperativeness of the family, the type of information that is needed, and the mandate of the therapist to treat the family as well as the child.

One technique I have used, which tends to get a great deal of information from families while meeting with a minimum amount of resistance, is what I call a "Psychological Scavenger Hunt." This "game" is best presented in a meeting with the whole family, but it can also work when presented to only one parent who then explains the game to the absent family members. The game is played like any other scavenger hunt, except that the scavenger lists are given to each family member and contain psychological items to bring into therapy.

A sample list might include:
1.   Something that makes you feel good about the family.
2.   A picture of a family member whom you don't see very often.
3.   A souvenir from a family trip.
4.   Something that causes fights in the family
5.   A picture that someone in the family made.

This technique can easily be varied according to the type of family that the therapist is seeing. With a motivated family, you can give a different list to each family member, and, like in a real scavenger hunt, give the family a time limit in which to obtain the items. The motivated family will enjoy the competition and bring enthusiasm and energy into the game. With an unmotivated family, the therapist may wish to give only one list to the whole family and appoint one person in charge of making sure that the therapeutic assignment is completed. With the former strategy, anyone who completes his or her list within the allotted time (either a specific time period, such as a Saturday afternoon, or the week between therapy sessions) will be declared a winner. With the second strategy, the whole family is declared a winner if the list is completed.

In the therapy session, the family presents all the objects to the therapist, who is the judge, explaining the relevant history or meaning of each one and coincidentally providing the therapist with a tremendous amount of diagnostic information. The therapist can vary this technique by his or her selection of items on the scavenger list; for example: items that evoke positive feelings, items that focus on specific family relationships, symbolic items, and so forth.

#10. Guaranteeing the Success of a Token Economy Chart by Adding Game Points

Theory: *Behavior Modification; Therapeutic Games*

Children with specific behavioral problems are often put on token economy programs where they win points by performing specific behaviors. Like any behavioral technique, the token economy point system is effective when the behavior is emerging; in other words, the child is both capable of performing and willing to perform the behavior but needs an extra push in his or her motivation. But what about the child who lacks specific behavioral or social skills, such as the ADHD child? Or the child who is only marginally motivated to change his or her behaviors, such as the aggressive child? These children typically have difficulty in winning points on a token economy system, and since they are then not rewarded, frequently give up trying altogether.

One way to help children succeed is by letting them win additional points by playing therapeutic games. In playing a published game (see Childswork/Childsplay catalog, 135 Dupont St., Plainview, NY 11803, 1-800-962-1141) or a therapist-made game (see *Short-Term Therapy with Children*, Childswork/Childsplay, LLC 1994), children can win chips or points which can be added to their token economy chart. Ideally, the game will also teach behavioral or social skills related to the objectives in the token economy system.

For example, The Classroom Behavior Game teaches children to wait their turn, raise their hands to be called on, listen to directions, and so on. Children can win points by answering questions pertaining to these skills in the game and by actually doing these behaviors in real life. The game gives children additional chances to win points which can be added to their token economy chart, ensuring success! Winning points by playing a therapeutic game gives children an opportunity to succeed that might not otherwise be available to them.

Figure 4.B
Token Economy Plus Game Chart

	M	Tu	W	Th	F	Sa	Su	Total
Doing homework								
Being polite								
Doing chores on time								
Not teasing the baby								
Showing good table manners								
Points (chips) won at games								
Totals								

By adding points to a token economy chart that children can win in playing a game, you allow the child to be more successful in a shorter period of time.

Motivating a Family with Behavioral Charts
#11. Chores Chart
#12. Problem-Solving Chart
#13. The Family Focus Chart

Theory: *Behavior Modification; Strategic Family Therapy*

Behavioral charts can be used not only to help motivate individual children towards behavioral change, but they can be used to motivate parents and whole families to change their behaviors as well.

There are two general types of charts that can be used with a family. The first takes a Family Systems point of view, treating all family members as equals and assuming that each family member has something that he or she should change. An important goal of Family Systems Therapy is to depathologize the identified patient and redefine therapy as more than a single person's problem.

A Chores Chart is a good example of how a family can be taught that each family member has specific responsibilities that contribute to the good of the whole. This weekly chart should include everyone living in the household (even children as young as four can do simple chores) and define specific chores or responsibilities that each person must perform. Specific privileges, such as dessert after dinner or TV time, can be contingent on the successful completion of each of the chores.

A Problem-Solving Chart is similar to the Chores Chart in its format; however, the tasks the family members must perform are determined with the aid of the counselor or therapist. For example, suppose there is an excessive amount of fighting in a family. The teenage girl keeps breaking her curfew and fights with her mother. The nine-year-old boy doesn't do his homework and his grades are poor. The parents fight over how to handle their children and also squabble over everyday pressures and problems.

The therapist might prescribe multiple therapeutic homework assignments to the respective family members and then use the Problem-Solving Chart to keep track of whether each task is accomplished. It is important that each

CHORES CHART

WEEK OF _____

WHO	WHAT	WHEN							DONE
		MON	TUES	WED	THUR	FRI	SAT	SUN	

family member agree to do his or her task, and the therapist must feel that each family member will live up to that agreement. In this example, the father might be responsible for convening and chairing a family meeting once a week, the teenage girl might agree to make the family dinner on a specific night, the son might agree to wash his parents' cars on Saturday, and the mother might agree to take over the task of paying the family bills and balancing the checkbook, which the father dislikes.

You will note that in this example, none of the tasks assigned to the individual family members directly deals with any particular problem. A systemic view of the family tries to change relationships and structural issues rather than directly addressing the presenting problems (which one assumes would be met with tremendous resistance). The tasks are chosen to address the underlying issues of cooperation and interdependence. Like in the Chores Chart, a specific privilege might be contingent on the completion of each family member's task.

A second direction for family behavioral charting comes more from the Behavioral School of Psychology than from Family Systems. Called the Family Focus Chart, this chart focuses directly on a particular problem that the child in therapy is having and needs to change, but it also stresses how other family members can aid in that child's change.

For example, suppose an ADHD child has two behavioral goals: finishing his homework and completing his chores on time. His older brother might be added to the behavioral chart as a daily tutor to the ADHD child. The father might be added as the person who can supervise the ADHD child with his chores. And the mother might be added as a person who can provide special playtime with the child, which is designed to foster his self-esteem. Each person on the chart would then earn points which can be "cashed in" for a predetermined reward, just like the child who is in treatment.

PROBLEM-SOLVING CHART

WEEK OF _____

WHO	WHAT	WHEN							DONE
		MON	TUES	WED	THUR	FRI	SAT	SUN	

FAMILY FOCUS CHART

WEEK OF _____

WHO	WHAT	WHEN							DONE
		MON	TUES	WED	THUR	FRI	SAT	SUN	

Techniques to Enhance Communication

Communication is the foundation for all forms of therapy. Whether it is in the therapy room, the home, the school, or with peers, people can be taught better ways to communicate which will not only address the presenting problem of the child, but will foster more meaningful and productive relationships as well.

Puppets in Therapy
#14. Animal Puppets with Traumatized Children
#15. Family Puppets
#16. Self-Esteem Puppets

Theory: *Values Clarification; Family Therapy*

Puppets have long been a staple in the therapy playroom as a way for children to take a voice other than their own. Some therapists prefer to use animal puppets, particularly with children who have been traumatized or are reluctant to reveal their feelings for some other reason. Speaking in the voice of an animal puppet, as opposed to a human puppet, seems to give these children a more comfortable psychological distance from which to communicate.

Typically, therapists set out eight to ten different animal puppets from which the child can choose. These puppets are chosen to provide different metaphoric representations for the child, and might include: a turtle (timid, protective); a lion (brave); a puppy or kitten (cute, vulnerable); an owl (wise); a monkey (silly, playful); a skunk (smelly, antisocial); a large animal like a dinosaur, elephant, or gorilla (powerful); a monster (scary); and so on. Most therapists initially give children complete freedom in choosing a puppet and in starting the puppet play. With very shy or inhibited children, the therapist might have to take the first puppet, or even take two puppets who will then have a dialogue. More directive therapists will ask the child (or group of children) to put on a puppet show, providing a stage, writing a storyline, and even videotaping each "play."

Family therapists often prefer a set of family puppets to help people enact various scenarios from the family, often taking the role of someone other than themselves. Family puppets can be obtained from Learning Resources, Inc., 675 Heathrow Drive, Lincolnshire, IL 60069; (800) 222-3909, as well as other suppliers. Family members are usually eager to take the role of someone else; sometimes too much so. They will tend to parody or caricaturize each other, and the therapist should be aware that this technique could bring out emotions or issues the family might not be ready to handle.

The therapist should keep control of the situation by being a strong "director" and setting some ground rules for the puppet play. For example, family members could be directed to exaggerate the "bad" and "good" features of the person (puppet) they are representing. The therapist should make it clear that these are exaggerated perceptions and not based on reality. The more volatile the family situation, the more the therapist will need to structure the situations by giving clear initial instructions and by coaching family members when they stray from these instructions. These could include:

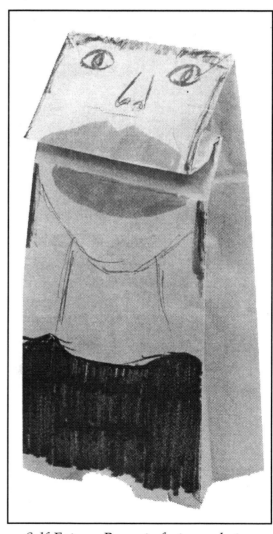

- Have your puppet speak in a way that shows the best part of that family member.

- Have your puppet speak in a way that you would like the family member to act.

Self-Esteem Puppets feature what a person is most proud of.

- Pretend your puppet has to go away for a month to camp, or on a business trip, or leave for some other good reason.

- Have your puppet say goodbye to each of the other puppets in a positive way.

- Have your puppet communicate to another puppet without using words.

By the initial instructions that the therapist gives, the family can be oriented towards expressing positive feelings, airing concerns, empathizing with each other, communicating more effectively, and so on.

Puppets can also be made out of a variety of materials to focus on a particular therapeutic task. For example, self-esteem puppets can be made using brown lunch bags, a dark marker, and crayons. Family members can be told, "Make a puppet of yourself that emphasizes the best part of you."

When this technique is used with a family, many parents draw a large heart on their puppet or represent their ability to be a good listener by drawing big ears. Children are usually more literal and when unassisted draw a baseball cap if they are good at that sport or draw themselves holding a video game control box. The therapist can aid the young child in drawing the puppet, emphasizing that he or she is to draw in some special quality that he or she has inside him or her rather than a thing or an interest.

Once the puppets are drawn, the family can be asked to try to solve a problem by speaking as their puppets, but emphasizing the best part of themselves that their puppets represent.

#17. Therapeutic Teddy Bears

Theory: *Developmental; Interpersonal/Communication*

There is a magical quality to teddy bears. They seem to represent for children (and many adults) a source of comfort, nurturance, and protection. For some children, they are a "transitional object" – a personification of the security that comes from an all-knowing, all-giving parent.

The people at Spinoza (1876 Minehaha Ave. W, St. Paul, MN 55104-0102; (651) 644-7251) have taken this concept of the teddy bear and further elaborated on its therapeutic properties. Spinoza the Bear (named after the famous philosopher) is a large cuddly bear whom the designers have fashioned in the shape of a Buddha. More important than his namesake or physical appearance, this bear talks and sings! Inside his tummy lies an easily accessible tape recorder. When you turn the red button on Spinoza's heart, he tells stories and sings endearing songs which deliver therapeutic messages to children suffering from a variety of physical and psychological problems.

Spinoza is a wonderful bear, but you can make your own speaking stuffed animal very easily. Choose any large plush animal, perhaps one that has some particular meaning to the child (the wise owl, the brave lion, etc.), and attach a backpack or cloth sack to hold a tape recorder. When the tape player is on, the animal comes to life, speaking in the prerecorded voice of a parent, playing lullabies, telling therapeutic stories (taped by the parent or therapist), teaching relaxation strategies, taking the child through guided imagery, etc. This magical animal can be exactly the kind of therapeutic friend the young child needs.

#18. 15 Minutes of Play – Every Day

Theory: *Client-Centered Play Therapy; Parent Training*

Over the last 20 years, there have been many programs designed to train parents in play therapy techniques. My own belief is that parent-child play has the potential to achieve therapeutic goals in four main areas: to enhance emotional communication between parent and child; to enhance the bond between parent and child; to teach values to children; and to teach specific emotional and social skills.

Play therapy, of course, was invented as a way for children to communicate their needs, desires, and conflicts. Understanding that children could not put their feelings into words, the pioneers of play therapy learned to observe and interpret the play of children for its metaphoric meaning. The second generation of play therapists, working in the 1960s and 1970s, saw that client-centered play therapy, which was designed to reflect back the meaning of a child's play, could also be extremely beneficial to the therapeutic process. Several model programs have shown that both parents and paraprofessionals can readily learn this type of play therapy, as long as the adult has a basic caring and nonjudgmental attitude towards the child. The obvious advantage of teaching this technique to adults in the child's life, rather than seeing it as the sole province of the professional counselor, is that it can be done more frequently and in a more natural setting.

My prescription for helping children with emotional problems (as well as for preventing problems) is 15 minutes of play a day. This time period seems to be both realistic for parents and paraprofessionals, and it is also sufficient to make an impact on a child's emotional development when done regularly. To begin , I teach parents to use client-centered play therapy to communicate better with their child. I explain how the acronym P.R.I.D.E. can help them remember the five principles of this type of play therapy:

- Praise your child for actions showing emotional or behavioral growth.
- Reflect what you think he is feeling as he plays.
- Imitate the way that he plays, to show him that you are paying attention and that you are able to meet him at his level.
- Describe what you see, which will help put words to his behavior and will also give him an opportunity to give you feedback.
- Educate him when he reveals inaccurate or dysfunctional beliefs. For example, if a child says, "Nobody likes me at school. Everybody thinks I'm stupid." Point out that "everybody" doesn't think the same thing. Say something like: "Some people may like you and some people may not like you. That is the way it is with children and adults. Try to spend time with the people who like you."

#19. A Computer Program That Talks to Children about Therapeutic Principles

Theory: *Cognitive Restructuring*

Recently, while reviewing computer graphics and drawing programs for children, I came across a fascinating program called Kid Works™ Deluxe (Knowledge Adventure, 4100 West 190th St., Torrance, CA 90504; (800) 545-7677), which is available at almost any store that carries a selection of educational software. Kid Works is a story-telling program that allows you to easily combine text and pictures, but the novelty of the program is that once the story is written, the computer will read it aloud!

Since the introduction of the first computer for commercial use, people have been fascinated with the idea that some day (perhaps sooner than we think) computers will talk to us, advise us, and even take care of us. With Kid Works (and you) part of that fantasy has become a reality. You simply type in any message, press the "speak" button, and your computer will read what has been written. Imagine all the things that you can do with a talking computer:

- Make a list of rules for a child. The computer will remind the child of the rules at the click of the button.

- Pretend the computer is the child's "secret," robot friend. You type in the "therapeutic," messages, but the computer speaks them.

- Shy or reticent children can have the computer talk for them. The computer's "stories" or messages can then be printed for a permanent record.

The Kid Works program was designed for children to use, and it is very simple to learn. Just type in your story, click your cursor on the symbol for "speak," and the computer reads whatever you have written. If it doesn't recognize a word and reads it with the wrong pronunciation, you can teach it that word in less than a minute. For example, I wanted the computer to say "Hi," but it read the word as "Hee." I told the computer (that is, I typed

31

into a dialogue box) that when it sees "Hi," it should read it as "high." From that point on, the computer has been always right when it reads "Hi."

If a child has a computer compatible with yours, at home or at school, you can write stories or messages for the child's computer to tell him, simply by giving him a disk with a copy of your story (of course, the child's computer would need to have Kid Works installed as well).

#20. Books as Therapy

Theory: *Bibliotherapy; Family Therapy*

Twelve years ago, when I first began researching a book on short-term therapy for children, I had only a lackluster interest in the technique of bibliotherapy – helping children deal with their problems through books. When I think back now to my lack of enthusiasm for this technique, I can attribute it to an ironic misconception about the nature of psychotherapeutic techniques: bibliotherapy seemed too easy to be true.

Having originally been trained in psychoanalytic methods, I held fast to the idea that dealing with any psychological issue involved first understanding the complex nature and workings of the unconscious as well as the conscious concerns. Having gone on to be trained in developmental theory, family therapy, social learning theory, and more, I saw children and their systems as being so richly complicated that I must have found it almost unacceptable that something as simple as reading a book could be of help.

But this was faulty thinking on my part. Since that time, I have seen and heard of many examples where children have been profoundly influenced by therapeutic books, and now I believe that this is one of the most effective techniques in a child therapist's arsenal. Steve de Shazer (*Keys to Solutions in Brief Therapy*, W.W. Norton, Inc., 1985) offers a nice analogy to explain how simple techniques can solve complicated problems. Dr. de Shazer believes that people have the solutions to their problems in their repertoire of behaviors, but those solutions are behind locked doors, and without some intervention, they remain inaccessible. The locks that keep us away from these solutions may be very complicated, but the keys that unlock the doors need not be. Interventions can be like "skeleton keys," and these keys can fit even the most complicated of locks.

Therapeutic books can take a number of forms, including: metaphoric books like fables and fairy tales, realistic books about children facing and coping with real problems, informational books that explain problems to children and offer solutions, and workbooks that provide interactive experiences for children to learn "psychological skills" much like they would learn academic skills.

Therapeutic books can be read by children or with children. Books are a vehicle for the family therapist to bring different members of a family together in reading a book, setting the stage for interaction and discussion around a particular theme or topic. I remember one case where I prescribed a book on divorce to the mother of a six-year-old who refused to talk or even listen about her parents' separation. The child literally covered her ears and shut her eyes whenever I or her mother started in on the subject. I instructed the mother to simply leave the book (which was written very simply and was illustrated by young children) on the table in their den and to pick it up and read it to herself several times a week. I also emphasized to the mother not to make any effort at all to force the book on her daughter. I assumed that the child's curiosity would eventually get the best of her, and in her own good time she would at least look at the book.

Although we never found out if the child ever looked at the book, the intervention was undoubtedly successful. The child's mother got tremendous comfort from reading and rereading this book. She reported that it made her feel like she was doing something to help her daughter. It made her feel less alone, and it assured her that there were many people like her who were dealing with a similar situation. And the book reassured her that in time, by facing problems realistically, the pain of the divorce would go away.

Therapists will undoubtedly find many uses for therapeutic books. Two sources for selecting or making therapeutic books for children are: Childswork/Childsplay, LLC, 135 Dupont St., PO Box 760, Plainview, NY; (800) 962-1141, and *Homemade Books to Help Kids Cope* (Brunner/Mazel, 1993). Once specific books have been identified, therapists can ask their local bookstores or libraries to stock these books, making them readily accessible to patients.

#21. Making Illustrated Therapeutic Books Without an Ounce of Artistic Talent

Theory: *Bibliotherapy*

There are hundreds, if not thousands, of books that address the psychological issues of children, and yet that still may not be enough. The problems of any given child are unique to him or her, and no published book can take into account the complexity of an individual child's life or lifestyle. But there is one way to have a therapeutic book that exactly addresses a particular child's needs or concerns – write it yourself!

Books written by therapists for a particular patient are almost always effective on some level. Not only do they provide the exact therapeutic messages and information that will help the child and his or her family, but they convey an unspoken message from the therapist to the child and family as well: "I care about you a great deal. I am willing to take the time and energy to create something just for you, which you can have with you for as long as you like." Books made for a child are also a tangible representation of the therapeutic process. They can be read and reread, shown to others, stored in a special place, and kept for years.

However, despite the relative ease and effectiveness of this technique, few therapists or counselors take the time to make therapeutic books for children. Many therapists like to use art techniques, but they are hampered by their own lack of artistic abilities, or they may see this process as too time-consuming. Fortunately, the computer has solved that problem for many of us. There are now many inexpensive programs that offer tens of thousands of clip art and photographic images for use on any computer. These images can be imported into word processing or drawing programs that are now standard when you buy most computers.

A sample page created with clip art.

35

A child can be asked to browse through clip art programs and then select images of interest to him. The therapist can then direct the child on how to create a picture using various images, and to tell a story about it. The drawing and story can then be used as a starting point for discussion or they can be interpreted as a "projection" of the child's emotional needs, desires, and conflicts. Including a child in the writing of a therapeutic book is a good way to summarize and reinforce important things that have been learned in any particular therapy session.

#22. Keeping a Feelings Diary

Theory: *Humanistic Psychology; Client-Centered Therapy; Bibliotherapy*

The Feelings Diary is another book that can be created to help children develop new psychological skills and coping strategies. Nearly all therapists assume that children who are able to talk about their feelings are less prone to acting them out and have a greater chance of having their needs met and their concerns addressed. But many times we neglect the important task of giving children the opportunity to develop a vocabulary of their feelings and to practice discussing and reflecting on their emotions.

One way to do this is by having the child take a blank book and make a daily entry of how he felt that day. He will need an age-appropriate list to refer to for his feelings vocabulary and to stimulate his daily entries (see the illustration on the next page). Each day, preferably with a parent, the child should write down important feelings that he had during that day on the top of the page. The child can then write (or dictate) the things that happened that brought on those feelings. Pictures can be drawn or magazine cut-outs can be added to illustrate the feelings.

The Feelings Diary should be kept for a minimum of 14 consecutive days, and then it can be done less frequently. The child may be encouraged to make an entry after a particularly hard day, in anticipation of a significant event, at a fixed time interval (e.g., the first Monday of the month), at significant calendar events (e.g., holidays, birthdays), and so on. With each entry, the parent or another nurturing adult should be available to encourage the child to explore his feelings and to act as a sounding board for the child. The most appropriate stance for the adult helping a child with this technique is to be nondirective: to listen and reflect the child's feelings, but to avoid correcting or even suggesting solutions to the child. A good resource for parents to learn this technique is *How to Talk So Kids Will Listen and Listen So Kids Will Talk* by Adele Faber and Elaine Mazlish (Avon Books, 1980.)

FEELINGS FACES

upset	satisfied	interested	loving	affectionate
stressed	bored	pleased	thoughtful	shocked
dreamy	guilty	sick	silly	excited
embarrassed	shy	surprised	confused	smart
irritable	lonely	anxious	brave	disappointed
jealous	peaceful	tired	proud	worried
mad	happy	sad	scared	

#23. "Talking Shirts" as a Communication Aid

Several years ago, I was working with a couple who simply never said what was on their minds. They only said what they thought the other person wanted to hear, and so naturally they each felt misunderstood. It occurred to me how many times adults and children need to be heard, but for a variety of reasons (inhibition, pride, social stigma) they don't say what is on their minds, and, in particular, how they feel.

I thought that if we just had an easy way to tell people how we feel, we would have a better chance of getting other people to communicate on an appropriate emotional level and help fulfill our emotional needs. That's when I got the idea for Talking Shirts. Talking Shirts are T-shirts I had printed up which showed a silhouette of a person on the chest, and the words: "Please remember that today I feel _____. The idea was for the child or adult to draw how he or she felt that day (using washable markers) and write the word or phrase that described his or her feelings. This struck me as a particularly good idea for people who have difficulty expressing or controlling their feelings.

On several occasions, I gave these shirts to patients with interesting results; as it turned out, the adults liked them better than the children. I gave one to a patient's mother who was suffering from a manic/depressive disorder. Her medication was sometimes effective and sometimes not, and she felt guilty that she inflicted her mood swings on her two children. Since her own cognitively based therapy

Talking Shirts are a novel way to enhance family communication.

38

(conducted by another therapist) was helping her recognize early warning signs of her mood swings, she liked using a Talking Shirt to remind her that other people needed to know her emotional state as well.

She wore the shirt several times a month when she felt that her emotional state was beginning to overwhelm her and she wanted her family to know. The family generally responded with a great deal more understanding than when this mother was unable to communicate her "early warning signs."

#24. Family Meetings

Theory: *Strategic Family Therapy; Family Systems Therapy*

Family meetings are a useful technique to enhance communication skills in children. Sometimes counselors make the mistake of prescribing family meetings in a casual way, as if this was an easy thing for parents to do. But most families who come for help with a specific problem also have a problem with general communication. Simply saying, "Why don't you have a regular family meeting," will be asking parents to do a difficult task without the necessary guidance.

Family meetings are most effective prescribed on a weekly basis. Ask parents to set aside a specific time, and to take about a half an hour for the meeting. Like any good meeting, there should be an agenda and rules. It is also important for parents and children to recognize that a family is not a democracy, where the majority vote determines important decisions. Parents should seek their children's input on every issue, but must ultimately retain the power for making appropriate decisions.

In families where there are multiple problems, it is usually a good idea to have one or two initial family meetings in the therapist's office. The therapist might help formulate the ground rules for the meeting, but should then step back and act in the role of a coach. An evaluation form, used at the end of the meeting, will also help the therapist monitor the effectiveness of the family meeting as a psychotherapeutic technique. This brief form should be filled out by all family members and used to see whether each person feels the meeting was useful in resolving problems and improving communication.

#25. Secret Sign Language

Theory: *Interpersonal/Communication*

Children love to have a secret language. It makes them feel special and powerful. It also has the advantage of bringing people together who know the secret language; after all, what good would a secret language be if there was no one else who understood it?

In the early 1980s, I ran a school for multiply-handicapped children and used some simple sign language to communicate with a group of students with various expressive language problems and moderate intellectual handicaps. At the same time, I was working with an ADD child in my private practice and was consulting with the child's teacher to help her with classroom management.

The teacher was very cooperative, but she was also tired of continuously reminding her student to pay attention or be quiet and felt that these constant verbal reminders also disrupted her class. The child wanted to improve his behavior, but unfortunately, like many ADD children, he still needed constant external feedback.

I asked the teacher and the boy if they would like to learn a secret language that would make it easier. I taught them both ten signs and asked the teacher to try to use each sign every day for several days to train her student to pay attention to her gestures. After several weeks, the student and teacher met and eliminated some of the signs that were not helpful and added a few secret signs of their own. The teacher used this special sign language for the remainder of the year and reported that it not only gave her a "language" to teach her pupil self-control, but it helped her develop a more positive feeling toward the student and his problems.

#26. Secret Codes for Secret Messages

Theory: *Communication/Interpersonal*

One principle that all child therapists learn early in their training is to "take the child where he is," meaning that the therapist should develop a full

A	B	C	D	E	F	G	H	I
∞	@	👁	⊏	▢	⌇	D	▽	÷

J	K	L	M	N	O	P	Q	R
~	≡	∅	⊡	‖	▽	+	⋈	=

S	T	U	V	W	X	Y	Z
◁	♡	△	⊟	∝	↔	⌀	‖‖

A	B	C	D	E	F	G	H	I

J	K	L	M	N	O	P	Q	R

S	T	U	V	W	X	Y	Z

understanding of the child's unique personality and behavior and build a therapy program from there. If possible, therapists should use the child's natural interests and abilities as a jumping-off point for therapeutic interventions.

Having worked with latency-age children in many different settings over the years, I frequently turn to one of their favorite themes (and mine) – the secret agent. I have used all kinds of secret codes to communicate with children in session and have recommended codes as a way for parents and teachers to have a special communication with a child as well.

One of the easiest codes to use is the "Secret Translator." Take two strips of paper with the alphabet printed on it, as shown on the previous page, and designate a symbol for each letter. You can use the symbols printed on the translator, or the child can make his or her own symbols. The person who writes the secret message and the person who reads the secret message will each need the same translator.

Once the translator is made, it can be used to encourage children to communicate in ways and about subjects they might normally resist:

- The child can write a coded message about something that has upset him or her.

- A teacher can write a special assignment in code.

- Parents can write a chores assignment in code.

- A child can get a coded message from an important person in a letter.

In each of these cases, the child will enjoy the bond that having a secret way of communicating always brings.

#27. Cartoon Reminders

Theory: *Client-Centered Therapy; Family Therapy*

How To Talk So Kids Will Listen and Listen So Kids Will Talk by Adele Faber and Elaine Mazlish (Avon Books, 1980) is one of the most popular parenting books ever published. Based on the work of Haim Ginott, the book takes a highly practical and yet humorous approach to teaching parents to be "reflective listeners." The book also takes a direct and organized stance in teaching these parenting skills, but what stands out in particular are the cartoons that show both the ways parents sometimes "negatively" respond to their children as well as positive ways in which they can communicate instead. The authors have noted how many of their fan letters describe how parents cut out these cartoons and post them around the house to remind themselves of better ways to respond to, and interact with, their children.

The best and most popular cartoons have the ability to humorously examine human foibles, in ways that are both self-reflective and forgiving. Having parents "find themselves" in the newspaper comic strips is an interesting way to help them get in touch with their common human behavior or the behavior of family members. It simultaneously forces them to be introspective and to "lighten up" about their problems.

The following assignment can be given to a family as therapeutic homework: "Find a comic strip or panel that reminds you of a problem or issue that is present in your household." In giving this assignment, the therapist or family counselor is focusing the family towards a common goal, one which is more pleasant than directing them to "Have a family meeting and come in and tell me about what you see as your conflicts or concerns."

When the family members bring a cartoon or comic strip to the session, the therapist has an immediate jumping-off point for discussion. If family members warm to this technique, they could go on to make a scrapbook of their favorite "family comics," which might include pages for family comments, solutions, and drawings, as well as the original cartoons.

Diagnostic Techniques

Therapists or counselors too often view the diagnostic or assessment phase of therapy as antiseptic and rote. When I was a school psychologist, we classified our work into two parts: assessment (boring) and counseling (fun). Schools and mental health agencies reinforce this dichotomy by requiring psychologists or other psychometricians to come up with numbers and classifications so that each individual child can be placed upon the appropriate path of education and treatment. Diagnosis and assessment for the purpose of classification and programming will always be a necessary task, but that shouldn't mean that an ongoing assessment in a child's treatment can't include fun and "magical" moments.

In this section, I will describe several ways that fairly mundane assessment techniques can be made more interesting by making them into games, and I will also suggest other informal ways to get diagnostic information from children through their natural language of play.

#28. The Drawing Game

Theory: *Projective Drawing Tools*

Many therapists use projective drawings as a method of assessment both before and during therapy. The most commonly used drawing techniques are the Draw-A-Person Test, The House-Tree-Person Test, and the Kinetic Family Drawing ("Draw a family doing something"). These and other drawing techniques can be very revealing; however, many times children are reluctant to offer projective drawings due to general inhibition, a lack of interest in drawing, or embarrassment over their lack of drawing skills. Turning the therapist's request for projective drawings into a game where points and prizes can be won is a sure way to interest a child in this technique.

To play the Drawing Game, you will need a square piece of poster board (at least 5" x 5") and a plastic "arrow" from a game spinner. Using a compass or tracing around a round jar lid, draw a circle that almost covers the piece of poster board. Divide the circle into four equal parts and write the words

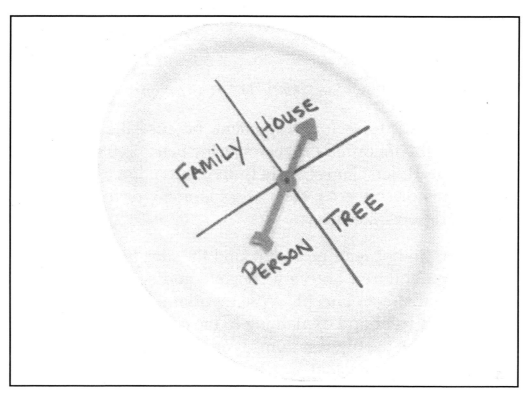

The Drawing Game is a way to motivate children to make projective drawings.

"House," "Tree," "Person," and "Family" in each part. Make a hole in the center of the circle and unsnap the plastic arrow and resnap it in the hole. If you don't have an arrow that comes apart, you can make a paper arrow and attach it with a pushpin.

Now tell the child that he has 10 spins to get the arrow to point to each of the four words and to produce the four pictures as indicated by the spin. He will get five chips for each picture he draws, which can be cashed in for stickers or other small rewards (e.g., 20 chips = a set of stickers). You will be amazed at how quickly children agree to do the drawings! In the unlikely event that the child doesn't get all four pictures in the 10 spins, you can simply play again, and he gets another 10 spins to complete the remaining pictures.

#29. Creating a Hierarchy of Fears with "The Ruler Game"

Theory: *Behavior Therapy; Systematic Desensitization*

Games are excellent tools for assessment, because the rules that define them can focus the therapist on very specific behaviors or information. I developed "The Ruler Game" to help me determine a hierarchy of the child's problems or concerns, such as a hierarchy of fears that might be used to begin desensitization.

Young children do not readily understand the idea behind a hierarchy or ranking. Young children are very concrete and so have a difficult time with this fairly abstract concept. When working with a younger child, I begin by taking a ruler and explaining to the child how the thing that she fears most would be the highest number on the ruler, the number 12. Then I ask her to tell me what that is. "Twelve is the highest number on the ruler, so it will represent your worst fear. Can you tell me what that is? What is the thing that you are afraid of most?"

I then ask her to tell me something else that she might be afraid of and ask where it would be on the ruler. Right in the middle at number six? Almost at the end, at number 10? Once she understands the basic concepts of ranking and hierarchy, I then tell her how "The Ruler Game" will help her remember all the things that she is afraid of and why this is important.

To play the game, the child simply has to drop the ruler with one hand and catch it with the other. The therapist then notes whatever whole number the child's index finger is closest to, and that is the "fear" that the child must identify. The game is over when the child has "caught" the ruler at all 12 numbers, identifying all 12 fears. (Note: This game can be made easier or harder by simply changing the distance that the ruler must fall before being caught.)

The Ruler Game can be played to help young children rank interests, problems, people they like, etc.

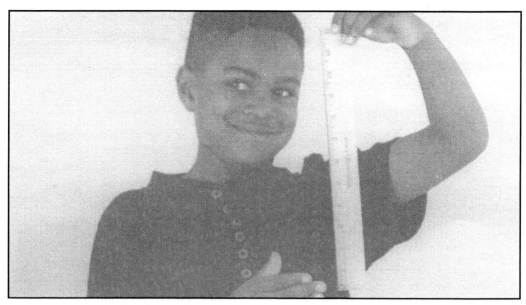

In The Ruler Game, the child uses a ruler to reveal a hierarchy of fears, needs, etc.

#30. Family Sociograms

Theory: *Family Systems*

Sociograms have frequently been used to get a schematic drawing of a family's interaction, but the information obtained for the sociogram is usually derived entirely from parental interviews. To get a child's point of view, you will need to use physical objects that represent the family members and the interactions between them.

A simple way to do this is by using checkers, pick-up sticks, and peel-off (pressure-sensitive) labels available at stationery stores. You will need both round and rectangular labels. You should have the rectangular labels in at least two colors.

Use one checker for each member of the family. Place a sticker in the middle of each checker and write in the name (i.e., Mom, Daddy, Joey, Pat, etc.) of each family member. On the pick-up sticks, attach labels with different verbal interactions that commonly occur in the family. Use one color for positive interactions and another color for negative interactions. For example:

Positive (Blue)	Negative (Red)
Hugs	Shouts
Drives (car)	Hits
Praises	Yells
Explains	Puts Down
Bandages	Punishes
Helps	
Kisses	

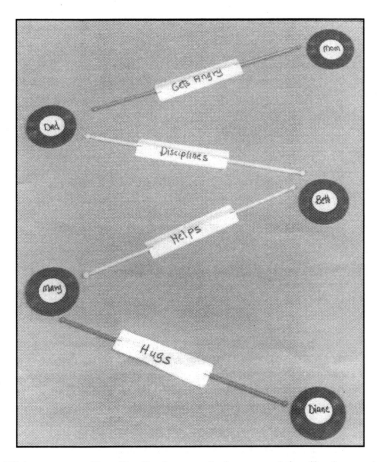

This concrete Family Sociogram helps reveal family dynamics.

Then ask the child to place a "stick" between the two people who have this type of interaction most often. You will quickly get a "snapshot" of the child's view of the intensity of the interactions between various family members, as well as how the child sees the degree of negative versus positive interactions.

#31. "Flinch:" A Game to Measure ADHD

Theory: *Developmental*

Games have a unique ability to aid in a therapist's ongoing assessment. Games can create an "experience" to observe a child along almost any developmental dimension. Often, when I want to know something about a child's behavioral, cognitive, or social skills, I make up a game to help me elicit that information from the child's perspective.

Flinch is a two-person, physical game that most of us played in childhood. One person holds both of his or her hands outstretched, palm-side up. The other person places his or her hands on top of the first player's hands, palms down. The first player must then try to "slap" the second player's hands. If he or she misses, then he or she continues to try. If he or she manages to slap

"Flinch" can help the therapist observe a variety of behaviors.

the other player's hands, then he or she gets to put his or her hands on top.

The therapist may only play this game for a few minutes with a child, but in this short time he or she will observe a variety of behaviors that can help in differentiating a child's impulse control, motor control, and propensity towards aggressiveness. Children with poor impulse control will have a very difficult time keeping to the rules. They may try to continue past the therapist's time limit, cheat, complain, and become overly aggressive (this will particularly happen when two children are playing together). Flinch and other physical games like Twister can also be used to teach children body control and how to keep their propensity for physical aggressiveness in check.

#32. Draw-a-Dream

Theory: *Psychodynamic; Family Therapy*

Dr. B. J. Tonge wrote about this simple projective technique in *The International Book of Family Therapy* (F. Kaslow, Editor, Brunner/Mazel, 1982). The therapist presents a picture like the one drawn on the next page to a child, with the statement: "Here is a picture of a boy named Bill (or some other name) having a bad dream. Maybe this boy is like you! Would you draw in a picture of what the boy might be dreaming about?"

It is assumed that the child will draw a picture reflecting problems that he or she is currently having. The therapist can then use the drawing to talk about real-life events that might have triggered the "dream," helping the child understand his or her feelings or behaviors around the conflict. Tonge suggests that the child be asked if he or she wants to show the picture to his or her parents who can then be involved in the solution.

Therapeutic Storytelling
#33. The Mutual Storytelling Technique
#34. Family Storytelling

Theory: *Psychodynamic*

The Mutual Storytelling Technique was developed more than 25 years ago by Dr. Richard A. Gardner as both a diagnostic and a therapeutic technique. Dr. Gardner is a firm believer in the power of stories to influence human behavior. From the first tales told around a campfire to the stories that form the basis of the Bible to fables and fairy tales, stories can both reflect and influence the laws and ethics of a culture as well as the day-to-day rules of behavior.

Dr. Gardner has developed a variety of games that can be used to elicit stories from children, including his published *Pick-and-Tell Games* which combines three storytelling techniques into a single board game (see *The Book of Psychotherapeutic Games*, Shapiro, 1994, for reviews). In playing these games, children make up stories after picking a toy, a word, or a picture of a person from The Bag of Toys, The Bag of Words, or The Bag of Faces. The child then tells a story using what he has selected from the bag as a stimulus and is asked to draw a lesson or moral based on that story.

For example, Bernard entered treatment at the age of seven-and-a-half due to his significant classroom behavioral problems. In his third session, he reached into The Bag of Toys, picked out a dog figurine, and told the following story:

> Once upon a time there was this dog. So this dog went away with his mas-
> ter. He was looking for hunting and they were hunting ducks...And when
> they came back he went to sleep...And after he woke up, he got a bone and
> then he, and then he went back to sleep again...Then he woke up and he
> went around with a boy...And he was walking him with the leash...And the
> boy hurt the dog...He had to go to the, the-he had to go where? Where's the
> place that dogs have to go when they're sick? (Therapist: Oh, a veterinarian?)

Yeah. He was pulling on the leash too hard and his neck started to hurt... And he fixed his neck up. And it took two days...And then he went back and he had a bone, another bone...And that's the end."

(excerpted from the instructions to *Dr. Gardner's Pick-and-Tell Games* by Richard A. Gardner, M.D.)

The above story was told with various prompts, questions, and clarifications by Dr. Gardner, which have been left out for ease of reading. In fact, this method of storytelling is more often a dialogue between the therapist and the client, rather than the telling of clear, distinct stories.

In this technique, the child gets three chips for telling the story. Dr. Gardner saw two themes in this particular story: the first related to the dog's preferred activity of sleeping, which Dr. Gardner interpreted as related to Bernard's passive attitude towards schoolwork and chores, and the second as an example of the boy's "magic-cure" fantasy, demonstrated by the dog's instant cure by the veterinarian. Dr. Gardner also points out that Bernard might have been depicting himself as the dog, indicating low self-esteem, being pulled by the leash of the boy, who might have represented his mother's strict and somewhat rigid demands.

When used diagnostically, the therapist would not respond with his or her own story, but would instead elicit more stories that would also be revealing of unconscious drives, needs, and conflicts. Dr. Gardner recommends that at least 11 or 12 stories be solicited to get a full diagnostic picture.

When used as a therapeutic technique, however, the therapist would alternately respond with a therapeutic story that would take into account the main pathological manifestation in the story, the primary inappropriate or maladaptive resolution of the conflicts presented, and an example of a more mature or healthier mode of adaptation than the one the child utilized.

In the above case, Dr. Gardner told a story in response about a boy and a dog who went out hunting. But when the dog suddenly decided to go to sleep, the boy admonished him. The dog went to sleep anyway, and when he awoke he asked his master for a bone; but the boy explained that if the dog had helped him with the hunting, he would have gotten a bone, but since he did not, he would get nothing. As they walked home, the dog had an accident and hurt his neck. But this time, the dog had to take medicine and do neck exercises in order to get better.

In this technique, the therapist's stories speak metaphorically to the child offering a powerful "window" into the unconscious developmental issues and conflicts. To learn more about this technique, read *The Psychotherapeutic Techniques of Richard A. Gardner, M.D.* (Creative Therapeutics, 1992).

Other therapists have adapted the Mutual Storytelling Technique for use with families. Using a stimulus like a toy, a word or a picture picked at random, a designated family member begins to tell the story. At the therapist's cue, the next family member then picks up the storyline and continues. The last family member must end the story.

As the story takes form, the therapist takes notes identifying where each family member begins and ends (or alternatively tapes the story). From a diagnostic viewpoint, family members may reveal their role in the family as problem creators or problem resolvers, cooperative or noncooperative, authoritarian or passive, and so on. The therapist may then offer a responding story, asking the family member to discuss why his/her story is different than the one presented by the family. Alternatively, the therapist may be more directive, calling upon specific family members to create problems within the stories and other family members to resolve the problems before the story ends. In this way, the therapist encourages family members to take on new roles and practice new skills within the family context.

Cognitive Techniques

Cognitive techniques have become increasingly popular with children because they can be implemented not only by therapists and counselors, but by teachers, paraprofessionals and parents as well. The "magic" in these techniques is in the way that they are introduced and applied with individual children. Like any kind of learning, cognitive techniques can be dull and repetitive, or they can be exciting and fun. In either case, the principles behind using these techniques will remain the same:

- Begin with a thorough understanding of a child's cognitive style.

- Take into consideration developmental, intellectual, and personality factors when choosing a technique.

- Be patient and consistent when implementing the technique.

- Always focus on applying the technique in real-life situations, since cognitive techniques often don't transfer or generalize to other situations.

#35. Cognitive Self-Instruction

Theory: *Cognitive Behavior Modification*

In *Attention Deficit Hyperactivity Disorder* (Guilford Publications, 1990), Russell Barkley details an interesting technique to help children with attention problems stay on task.

When a child has trouble staying on task, the adult can stand over his shoulder and give him an encouraging remark every five minutes or so. Or you can make a tape recording of encouraging remarks that can play as the child works. It is helpful to have a tape recorder with a "real time" counter, which can record the remarks at random intervals between 3 and 15 minutes apart.

Barkley notes that a father's voice seems to be particularly effective with ADD children, but another authority figure or a person important to the child could also be effective. Comments can be used to help a child develop independent skills, such as:

Motivation: "Keep trying. I'm proud of you!"

Concentration: "Keep your mind on your work now!"

Relaxation: "Take a break for a minute. Get up and stretch while you count to 60."

Self-Instruction
#36. Teaching Children to Follow a Schedule
#37. Using a Tape Recorder to Keep Children On Task

Theory: *Cognitive Behavior Modification*

Self-instruction teaches children a procedure for doing a particular task independently. This procedure emphasizes a concrete way for children to accomplish a task with minimal supervision, and it is particularly useful for children with poor time management and organizational skills due to a learning disability or attention deficit disorder. This technique teaches children the major components of independent work, including:

1. How to start the task

2. The specific stages of the task

3. Ways to stay on task until it is completed

Nightly homework is a task that children frequently have difficulty doing without close supervision. Taking the time to teach children independent study skills will not only have the immediate effect of improving their school performance and self-esteem, but it will also lay the foundation for study and work skills throughout their lifetime. The therapist or counselor begins by making a schedule of the task that is to be completed, detailing each step of the task:

1. Be at your desk at exactly 5:00 pm.

2. Clear your desk of everything but the homework you are doing.

3. Make sure there are no distractions.

4. Set your timer for 30 minutes.

5. Work until your timer goes off.

6. Set your timer again for five minutes and take a break (stretching or relaxing, but no reading, TV or phone calls).

7. Set your timer again for 20 minutes.

8. Work until the timer goes off.

9. Set your timer for 5 minutes. Use this time to check your work.

(From *The A.D.D. Tool Kit*, Gauchman, Wong, and Shapiro, Childswork/Childsplay, LLC, 1994)

This sequence should be written out and placed in clear view of the child as he or she works. The child should be required to read it aloud several times before beginning the homework and then several more times, saying it to him- or herself. Again, it is hoped that this systematic procedure will eventually be internalized in the child's thoughts and may then generalize to other similar situations, such as in-class work. However, even if this internalization doesn't take place, the child will be experiencing a systematic way of organizing his or her time.

An alternative for very impulsive or disorganized children would be to make a 55-minute tape recording, with the instructions occurring at the appropriate time on the tape. The tape would guide the child through the homework session. If you use a tape recorder, this would not take a long time. Simply record the schedule, such as the one listed above, at the appropriate time on the tape. In addition, the adult can add reinforcing comments on the tape as in the Self-Instruction Technique (#35).

#38. Naming the Disorder

Theory: *Cognitive Behavior Modification*

In working with Obsessive Compulsive Disorders (OCD) in children, Dr. John March urges his patients to put a name on their disorder. March credits Michael White, an Australian family therapist, for developing this technique of externalizing the problem in order to motivate children to deal with it more vigorously. Early on in the treatment, in the first or second session, March has the child or adolescent give his OCD a nasty nickname, emphasizing his reproach for this problem which is so affecting his life.

March tells of a child who developed OCD symptoms after being viciously berated by his teacher, Mrs. T. Afterward, the child developed tracing and retracing rituals and went from being an "A" to an "F" student. This child began referring to his OCD as "The Mrs. T. Problem."

March notes that children often use names like "Silly Worries" and "Terrible Troubles" when referring to their OCD. March notes that when children give their problem a name, it is the first step in distancing themselves from the problem and treating it as "the enemy." The techniques children learn to relinquish their OCD symptoms become weapons in their war against the OCD enemy.

In psychoanalytic terms, this cognitive technique is referred to as changing the symptom from being ego-syntonic to ego-dystonic, meaning that the symptom becomes detached from the patient as an acceptable part of his or her self-image, and involving the recognition by the patient that the symptoms are maladaptive and dysfunctional.

This technique could apply to children with simple phobias, nail-biting, hair-pulling, encopresis...any concrete symptom that the child needs to see as apart from him- or herself. In separating from the symptom, the child can muster his or her forces to attack "the enemy," and while diminishing the symptoms, he or she simultaneously improves his or her self-esteem.

The more the child's motivation to fight the symptoms is encouraged, the less the chance that the secondary gains of the symptom will influence the treatment.

Affirmations
#39. Overexposure to the Affirmation
#40. The "Me" Box
#41. An Affirmations Diary
#42. Parent Affirmations Diary

Theory: *Cognitive Behavior Modification; Humanistic Psychotherapy*

Affirmations are typically associated with the humanistic and self-help movements. They refer to positive self-statements that affirm one's sense of self-worth and value. The theory behind this technique assumes that adults (and children as well) have negative "scripts" or voices inside them that detract from their self-esteem. These "voices" may have originally come from negative criticism by significant others, or they could be self-originated. A prepubescent girl who sees fashion models and TV stars as role models says to herself, "I'm too fat, I'm disgusting." A boy with poor motor coordination says to himself, "I'm a spaz, nobody likes me." Wherever they come from, these negative self-statements at minimum lower a child's self-esteem and, at worst, contribute to serious psychopathology.

Affirmations are used as an answer to or substitution for these negative voices. It is assumed that if children learn to say positive things to themselves, it will help them cope with problems, be less affected by peer pressure, develop internal motivation, and develop a sense of self-worth.

Although affirmations are associated with the humanistic and self-help movements, they are essentially a cognitive-behavioral technique and, as such, are governed primarily by behavioral principles. In other words, positive self-statements will be learned most effectively when they are repeated often and reinforced frequently.

Teaching children positive self-statements seems like a straightforward and easy task, but simple techniques can be just as simply undermined. Several years ago, I was working with a learning-disabled boy, Sam, who had a very poor self-image. He felt that he was clumsy, unable to read well, and that his classmates disliked him (and, in fact, all three of these self-statements had some basis). With Sam's aid, we made a list of five positive things that he could say to himself:

1. I'm a kind and considerate person.

2. I'm good at Ping-Pong.

3. When I try hard, I can get good grades.

4. I keep my things neat and organized.

5. I give my toys away to poor children.

After the session, I gave Sam this list and asked him to memorize the five self-statements by the next week. When he came in the next week, however, I wasn't too surprised when he said that he had lost the paper. I gave him another list with the same instructions, but a week later, Sam returned empty-handed and again said he had lost them.

I realized this could go on for many weeks, and, in fact, that Sam's irresponsibility and lack of interest was a symptom of the very problem that I was trying to address. It was a self-fulfilling prophecy. I had no interest in getting caught up in Sam's cycle of defeat, so I decided to rely on an old behavioral trick of overexposure to the stimuli. I asked Sam's mother to come into the therapy room. While I explained the importance of positive self-statements to Sam and his mother, I made 500 copies of his list on the copier.

With his mother's approval, at the end of the session, I asked Sam to literally wallpaper his room with the copies of his list. At the next session, Sam and his mother reported that he had covered every inch of his walls, as well as his bathroom mirror and the ceiling over his bed, with his positive self-statements. Everywhere Sam looked he saw the five positive things that I wanted him to say to himself, and, needless to say, he had learned his lesson well.

The Me Box holds a month's worth of a child's personal affirmations.

The "Me" Box is another technique frequently used to encourage positive self-statements. Typically, the child decorates a shoebox or other small box with pictures, photographs, or other decorative items that reflect his or her interests or identity (e.g., a Girl Scout badge, ticket stubs from a play, a spelling quiz with an "A" grade, etc.). Then every day for at least a month, the child is asked to write something positive about himself or herself and put it in the box. For example:

"I washed my Mom's car today."

"My teacher said that I tried really hard."

"I got a home run and a double!"

When the month is up, or the box is filled, the "Me" Box is finished. It then serves as a reminder of the child's ability to think and act positively and it can be "reactivated" whenever the child may be having a difficult or stressful time.

A similar technique, appropriate for somewhat older children, is the Affirmations Diary. Using a blank book obtained from a stationery or gift store (or made by folding plain lined paper in half), the front of the diary is decorated with a favorite photograph of the child. Unlike other diaries, each entry can only be positive, describing a positive thought, event, image, or even a fantasy. The Affirmations Diary is a useful way to teach children the importance of positive thinking. Both anecdotal and empirical research have suggested that children who express a positive viewpoint about themselves and others are better liked by adults as well as by peers, and they are typically more successful in school and in other areas of their lives as well.

The Parent Affirmations Diary is also a useful way of reminding stressed parents to have a positive view of themselves and their parenting efforts. Many times children with serious problems not only require a tremendous amount of time, energy, and patience, but offer disproportionately little gratification to their parents. Parents of children with visible disabilities are often given a great deal of credit by society for their dedication. But parents

The Affirmations Diary stresses positive thinking.

of children with invisible problems, particularly those associated with problem behaviors (e.g., defiant children, children with attention deficit disorders, etc.), are less likely to be valued for the same level of parental effort. These parents may become depressed and stressed and may develop any number of symptoms or dysfunctional behaviors.

Just like the children for whom they care, parents may also benefit from learning to use affirmations or positive self-talk. They can keep an Affirmations Diary similar to the one described above, noting their daily positive efforts in raising their children. Sample entries might include:

> "Saturday, September 12. Today was hard. Johnny needed constant reminders to behave while we were shopping. But he didn't throw a tantrum, and that's an improvement!"

> "Sunday, September 13. Today I took three hours for myself. I sat in the tub for a whole hour and soaked away a week's worth of stress! Then I cooked a big family meal, with everyone's favorite foods."

The diary could serve as a way for the therapist or counselor to monitor how a particular parent is responding to his or her advice. It could be an assignment that focuses the parent on specific positive child-rearing techniques, including:

- Seeing progress in small steps

- Providing more positive than negative feedback

- Applying behavioral techniques (such as a time-out or a token economy system) consistently

- Providing "Special Time" for a child (see Technique #81) and so on.

The diary should be simple to do so that parents don't see it as a chore. One or two sentences each day will be enough. The creative parent could also add drawings, photographs, mementos of the day, etc.

#43. The Triple Column Technique: Teaching Children to Argue with Themselves

Theory: *Cognitive Restructuring*

There are two major categories of cognitive techniques: cognitive mediating techniques and cognitive restructuring techniques. Cognitive mediating techniques assume that the child has a specific cognitive deficit in the way she uses self-guiding thoughts and that this deficit impairs her behavior. For example, impulsive children do not use thoughts to mediate their behaviors. They do not plan ahead, use problem-solving, weigh decisions and so forth (see Technique #44 for an example of a cognitive mediating technique).

Cognitive restructuring techniques, on the other hand, assume that children and adolescents have an internal dialogue that guides their behavior, but the thoughts they have are often "irrational" or "dysfunctional." However, Aaron Beck, developer of the cognitive treatment of depression, and Albert Ellis, developer of Rational/Emotive Therapy, assume that much of our self-defeating behavior is governed by our dysfunctional thinking. Their therapies are both based on the idea that if you can change automatic dysfunctional thoughts, you can change the dysfunctional behavior as well.

The Triple Column Technique was developed by Beck and his colleagues at the University of Pennsylvania (*The Cognitive Theory of Depression*, Guilford Press, 1979) and is a simple form that can be used to help older children (above the age of 10), adolescents, and parents learn to recognize and change their automatic self-defeating thoughts. In introducing this technique, the therapist or counselor must first explain the nature of dysfunctional thoughts. They occur because of a variety of cognitive distortions, including:

Overgeneralization: "Everyone hates me."

Absolute thinking: "I'll never learn how to do long division."

Focusing on negative details: "My hair looks ugly. People will make fun of me."

Disqualifying positive occurrences: "Sharon asked me to her party, but that's because her mother made her ask everyone in the class."

Minimizing or maximizing the importance of occurrences: "I gave a really dumb answer in class today; now everyone will think I am stupid."

Overpersonalizing the reactions of others: "Dad never finds time to be with me. He must think I'm a big disappointment."

Once this has been done, the therapist should help the client identify his dysfunctional thoughts by having him talk about a particular problem by writing down any examples of self-defeating thoughts. These should then be placed in the first column of the form.

The remainder of the session will focus on identifying why these automatic thoughts are dysfunctional (column 2) and what would be a more rational response to these thoughts (column 3). In effect, this technique teaches the client to argue with him- or herself, identifying self-defeating statements and replacing them with realistic and positive ones, which will in turn produce more positive feelings and behaviors.

For example:

Automatic Thought	Cognitive Distortion	Rational Response
1. I'm all alone in the world.	This is the way I feel, but it is not really true.	I feel lonely, but there are many people I care about and who care about me. But I still feel I want more. There are things I can do about this.
2. I'm doing lousy in school. There is no reason to try and study harder and go to college.	I am maximizing my failures.	I'm doing poor in some subjects but well in others. Everyone has strengths and weaknesses.

Use this blank form for your purposes:

Automatic Thought	Cognitive Distortion	Rational Response

This technique can be used with parents as well as children and adolescents. Often, parents can be taught to deal more appropriately with their child's problems by helping them recognize their own automatic irrational assumptions and attitudes.

#44. Stop and Think, Then Proceed: Reducing Impulsivity in Children

Theory: *Cognitive Behavior Modification*

Some of the most difficult children we work with have problems in impulse control. In most cases, part of their treatment involves cognitive strategies that help them be more reflective and to literally "think before they act." Cognitive mediating techniques have been used for more than 20 years as a way of teaching children to use an internal dialogue to guide and control their behaviors. Researchers like Bonnie Camp at the University of Denver Medical School and Donald Meichenbaum at the University of Montreal have pioneered techniques to help children practice "reflective" cognitive skills.

The research conducted on these techniques has shown that they can be effective in office training, but they often fail to generalize to the child's natural environment where the impulsivity is occurring.

Recently the issue of generalizability of self-control training has been addressed by Dr. Kenneth Dodge, a professor at Vanderbilt University in Nashville, who is involved in a program researching children with conduct disorders called FAST TRACK. This program uses a very concrete way to help children stop and think about their behavior, using the model of a traffic light.

When children misbehave, they are immediately directed towards a "red light." This could be a literal red light, a red circle on the floor to stand in, or a red spot on their desk that they touch. When they are at the red light, they must count to 120, taking deep breaths in order to relax.

Next the child goes to a "yellow light" to think about what to do next.

Younger children may generate one solution, but older children may be directed to imagine different solutions and the consequences that might occur with each alternative.

Finally, the children go to a "green light" where they try out a solution to see if it works. If they hit someone, they would certainly have to apologize. If they took something, then they would have to make reparation, and so on.

What makes this technique so appealing?

1. It uses an effective yet flexible psychological principle.

2. It is concrete and can be applied effectively in the counselor's office, the home, or the school.

3. It has both cognitive and physical aspects. Children's emotional reactions are much more physical than adults, and this technique allows children to deal with their emotions in a physical as well as a cognitive way.

4. It is fun. It would be particularly fun if you used real "red," "yellow" and "green" lights for the child to go to. Going to the different lights and standing near them while the technique is performed reminds me of running to a base in tag or softball, which children of course enjoy.

This technique works on the metaphoric as well as the concrete level. The stoplight is something to which all children can relate as a symbol of adult traffic rules. The three types of lights represent stages, and as the child moves from one to another, he or she makes progress towards a higher stage of functioning.

Teaching and Enhancing Social Skills

Child psychotherapy has traditionally focused more on intrapsychic and family problems, but therapists or counselors should not neglect helping children with social and interpersonal problems as well. Children with specific diagnosable problems frequently have concomitant difficulties in their peer relationships. If they then have difficulty in making and keeping friends, this affects their self-esteem and deprives them of important opportunities for developmental and social learning.

Fortunately, there are many techniques available to the creative therapist to help children relate better to their peers, as well as to other people in their community. Because of the nature of social problems, the therapist will have to use other people in other settings to help the child develop new skills. The following techniques combine ideas that can be used in the office with those that will need to be implemented, or at least monitored, in the child's home, school, and community.

Teaching Social Skills Through Magic
#45. Magic as a Hobby
#46. The Mind-Reading Dice: Using Magic to Teach Friendship Skills
#47. Using Magic to Teach Children How to Give a Compliment: The Positive Attitude Rainbow
#48. Things Are Not What They Seem: The Magic Cauldron

Theory: *Cognitive; Behavioral; Developmental*

Magic tricks have been popular with many therapists as a way to engage and interest the child. Therapists often see themselves as "magicians," so why not use a few tricks? Sometimes therapists will use magic as a way to engage a child in therapy or to motivate him. A therapist may demonstrate a trick to a child and then show him the "secret" behind the trick as a reward at a later date.

But besides simply engaging children in therapy, magic tricks can be used to teach a variety of interpersonal skills. If you have ever performed any magic tricks yourself, you know that good magic involves a wide variety of cognitive and social skills, including:

- Telling a story (patter)

- Mastery (having learned something that other people don't know and then demonstrating it)

- Getting someone's attention in a positive way

- Making a "connection" with the audience

- Persistence (in practicing the trick)

- Self-control (in showing the trick)

- Problem-solving (if the trick goes wrong or the audience doesn't react the way you want them to)

A child's interest in magic might also be turned into a very appropriate "hobby" for children with attention problems, low self-esteem, antisocial behavior, etc. Anna Freud has emphasized the importance of hobbies in a child's growth, calling hobbies "halfway between play and work" and containing important elements of each.

Magic tricks can be very simple, like the examples listed on the following pages, or they can be quite complicated and therefore frustrating for children. The magic kits in toy stores tend to be much too complicated, particularly for children with emotional problems and limited frustration tolerance. Individual tricks that come with books like *The Party Magician Kit* (Watermill Press, 1993) or *Magic Fun* (edited by Marilyn Baille, Little, Brown and Co., 1992) or sold separately in toy stores should first be selected by an adult and then taught to the child (if the child is proficient at learning tricks, then additional tricks can be learned independently). Once the child has learned the trick, he or she should be encouraged to perform it for the adult.

Again, the social aspects of doing magic should be emphasized, including helping the child give an "entertaining" performance, helping the child develop a story to go along with the trick, and helping the child deal with the various reactions of the audience.

As a hobby, magic shares important developmental components with other hobbies enjoyed by children: collecting, organizing, demonstrating, learning the history of the hobby, identifying with other people who enjoy the same hobby, and even making money from the hobby! Once a child has mastered a dozen tricks or more, he or she may wish to "perform" as a magician at parties for younger children. Again, the performance should be looked at as a time to teach children important skills. Adults should help the child put the show together, rehearse the individual tricks, design a costume, and so on. A successful magic performance is really not much different from a piano recital; it requires the close supervision of an adult combined with the time and patience involved in practice.

The three tricks that follow not only provide the cognitive and social benefits of learning any magic trick, but they have been modified to emphasize a specific social skill as well.

The Mind-Reading Dice is an almost foolproof trick for children eight and older. The trick is based on a mathematical principle, and the child will have to be comfortable with subtracting two numbers in his or her head for the trick to succeed. All you will need to teach the trick are three ordinary dice, a piece of paper, and a pencil. If performing before an audience, the child magician will need an "assistant" to do the trick, but this trick will more likely be done with just a one-person audience. Here is how it works:

Magician: *This is a trick about mind reading. Mind reading is a way of knowing somebody so well that you can sometimes tell exactly what they are thinking.*

(If the magician knows the person, he says a few things that he already knows.) *For example, I know your favorite movie is "The Terminator." At your last birthday party, you served chocolate cake. And you have a cat named Snickers!*

(If the child doesn't know the assistant, he must ask some questions to get to know him.) *Let me ask you some things about yourself. How old are you? What is your favorite TV show? What Halloween costume did you wear last year?* (And so on). With each answer, the magician looks very thoughtfully and sincerely at his assistant. This can be practiced in a mirror.

Now, I am going to show you three dice, and I'm going to stack them one on top of another. If I look at this tower of dice, I can see most of the sides, but I can't see five of the sides. (Point out the five sides that can't be seen; see figure on the next page). *Now I want you to throw all three dice on the table and then stack them into a tower.* The assistant should do this.

All right, now I will turn my head and I want you to write down the five numbers on the five sides that I can't see, and then add them up so that you have just one number. The magician turns around and waits until the assistant has done this.

Now I am going to look into your eyes, and I want you to think of your number. Think very hard! Get a picture of the number in your brain and I will read it out loud ... concentrate ... concentrate ... 17! Your number is 17! Right! It's nice to know someone so well that you can read their mind!

The secret of this trick is very simple and relies on a fact that not too many people know. Everyone knows that a die has six sides, but they don't know that when you add one side of a die with its opposite side, the number always equals "7." (Check it out for yourself). Therefore when you stack the three dice, the total number for all six of the top/bottom sides must equal 3 times 7, or 21 (see illustration on the next page). To get the sum of the five hidden numbers, the magician need only look at the number on the top die, and subtract this from 21. In the above example, for instance, where the answer was 17, a 4 must have been showing on top.

This trick always works, but it must be practiced. When teaching this trick to a child, the therapist will have the opportunity to talk about the social aspects of getting to know someone so well that you can "read their mind." As in the dialogue above, this part of the "patter" should be emphasized. As the trick is taught, the importance of knowing about someone else can be discussed in terms of performing magic as well as enjoying all forms of social relationships!

In using magic to teach social skills, particularly to children who have significant problems in this area, I depart from the normal magician's code of "never tell how a trick is done." In fact, I take the opposite stance: I always tell how a trick is done! Sharing the secret behind a trick is like sharing any other important secret: it is a gift that creates a special bond between two people. Not sharing a trick, on the other hand, creates distance between two people, and a sense of "I'm better than you, because I know something that you don't." This is obviously counterproductive to teaching children to make and keep friends.

When I teach a trick to a child, before I perform the trick I tell him that I will teach it to him when I am done; and I encourage children to take this same approach when they perform tricks for children of the same age. (Note: The exception to this rule is when an older child shows a trick to younger one, typically a younger sibling. In this case, I think it's appropriate to withhold

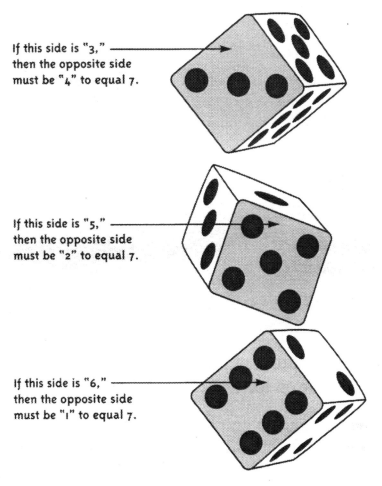

If this side is "3," then the opposite side must be "4" to equal 7.

If this side is "5," then the opposite side must be "2" to equal 7.

If this side is "6," then the opposite side must be "1" to equal 7.

the secret, because it keeps the older child in a more powerful position, which, from a developmental point of view, is where he or she should be.)

The Positive Attitude Rainbow trick is a simple trick and again almost fool-proof. It is based on an optical illusion. I introduce the trick by saying to the child: "When you think positively, you can do things you might have never thought you could. You can even touch a rainbow and stretch it." Having piqued the child's curiosity, I take just a few minutes to talk about positive thinking and how so many famous people have overcome different obstacles by seeing the positive things about their situation.

Then I do the trick.

To perform this trick yourself, make a copy of the rainbows on the next page and color them in brightly with crayons or markers. Now paste each one on an index card and cut it out.

To begin, simply place the rainbow with polka dots underneath the one with stripes.

> Say to the child: *I'm going to show you the power of positive thinking. I'm going to stretch this dotted rainbow and make it bigger than the one with stripes. To help me be strong, I'm going to say five really positive things about myself.*
>
> Then say five positive things about yourself, giving them some thought and elaborating as appropriate.
>
> *Now that feels good! I can feel myself getting stronger! Watch how I take the smaller rainbow and make it bigger!*

Lift up the rainbow with polka dots and pretend to pull hard on it. Then return it to the table, placing it above the striped rainbow. Voila! It is bigger!

The trick works because it is an optical illusion. Both rainbows are exactly the same size, but the rainbow on top always looks bigger.

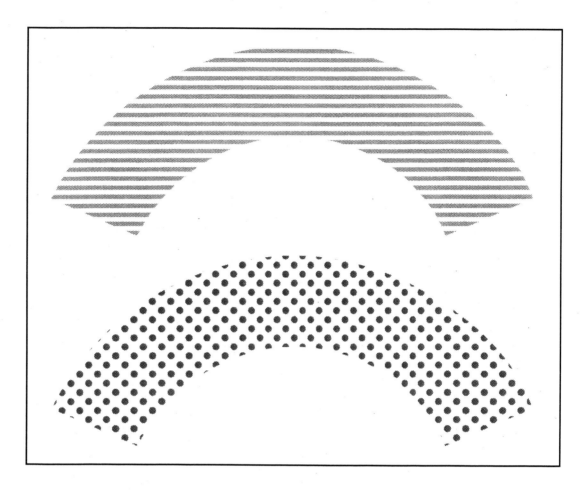

Now have the child do the trick, again emphasizing the part where he or she says positive things, explaining how the "story" behind every trick is what makes it interesting, and a story is always more interesting when it is true. Hopefully this will lead into a conversation about how positive thinking really can help you do wondrous things.

Encourage the child to show this trick to his friends and family, again explaining the "secret" after the trick is done. This puts the child in an interesting therapeutic position: teaching others to think positively!

The Magic Cauldron is a fun trick that teaches a simple lesson: Things are not always what they seem. The magician begins:

> *As you can see, I have an ordinary glass of water.* (The glass should be just half full.) *But with just a drop of my magic elixir and a pinch of my magic powder, I can turn it into a powerful potion that can be used to scare*

all the evil witches and bad monsters away. With that explanation, the magician adds a drop or two of blue liquid from a vial into the glass and some of her magic powder, and lo and behold, it bubbles and overflows!

The secret is simple: The water is really white vinegar and the magic powder is baking power. The blue liquid, of course, is just food coloring. This is fun to do over and over again. (Note: Put the glass on a large tray or you will have a considerable mess on your table). In discussing the "secret" of the trick, the therapist can talk about other things that are not as they appear, giving examples related to the child's problems or concerns.

Assertiveness Training for Children and Parents
#49. The Broken Record Technique
#50. Dealing with Criticism through Practice
#51. The Power of a Compliment

Theory: *Assertiveness Training*

Recently I was in line in a toy store behind an adorable but unhappy four-year-old girl and her mother. The child was wailing that she wanted a particular toy, and her mother was adamant that she shouldn't have it. Their conversation went like this:

Girl: But I just want this one thing! I'll be good, I promise!

Mother: You just got something yesterday, and the day before that! I can't keep spending money on you all the time! Today I am here for your brother and not for you.

Girl: But I just want this toy cat. I don't want anything else. Please ... please!

Mother: I said no, and I mean it. Now I am getting really mad. Do you want me to get you something in every store I go to?

Girl: No ... just this one thing ... I'll be good ... (crying louder) just this one thing, please, please!

This went on for perhaps five minutes (it seemed like 15), with the mother getting observably more angry and the child becoming more hysterical. Finally, when the mother was at the cash register and ready to pay, I was surprised that she used a new tactic:

> **Mother:** Okay. I can't stand it anymore. You want the cat, get the cat! Go get it! But I'm returning the ballet slippers and tights that I got you yesterday! Okay? Is that what you want?

> **Girl:** (wailing louder) I don't know! I can't choose! (The girl was now completely out of control, being faced with this dilemma.)

Finally the mother and her daughter left the store, without the toy, each feeling lousy. The mother banged her shopping cart around loudly to show her anger, and she grabbed her child roughly by the arm as they left.

Cynthia Whitman, M.S.W., might have suggested another tactic from her book *Win the Whining War and Other Skirmishes: A Family Peace Plan* (Perspective Publishing, 1991). Ms. Whitman refers to the type of behavior exhibited by this child as an example of "d.t.s," or diversionary tactics. The mother is trying to be firm, but her child keeps hooking her into an argument, raising the stakes. Children are good at this, and they often use this type of tactic as a reflection of their willfulness. Parents rarely win this type of argument because they get conflicted between their anger, their desire to please the child, and their feelings of being manipulated.

According to Ms. Whitman, the only way to win this battle is not to enter into it. She suggests a technique called the Broken Record Technique, which may also be familiar to those who do assertiveness training. In this technique, the parent simply repeats the same phrase, over and over again, no matter what the child does or says. In the above example, the mother might have said, "I'm sorry you can't get what you want today," repeating it over and over again as a response to the child's manipulative pleading.

Let's replay the scene, with the parent using the Broken Record Technique:

Girl: But I just want this one thing! I'll be good, I promise!

Mother: I'm sorry you can't get what you want today.

Girl: But I just want this cat. I don't want anything else. Please... please!

Mother: I'm sorry you can't get what you want today.

Girl: Just this one thing....I'll be good...(crying louder) just this one thing. PLEASE!

Mother: I'm sorry you can't get what you want today.

Girl: (crying more softly) But you never...

Mother: (more sympathetically) I'm sorry you can't get what you want today.

The mother and her child leave the store. The child is unhappy, but the "battle" has de-escalated. The mother feels good that her discipline has worked.

The Broken Record Technique can also be taught to children as a way to help them deal with peer pressure, teasing, or other negative situations. Take, for example, the boy who gets teased by the class bully:

Bully: You're a creep. Hey, you little creep.

Boy: I don't like being teased.

Bully: Oh, I bet you're a crybaby too! You little creep.

Boy: I don't like being teased.

Bully: You're an idiot. Is that all you can say?

Boy: I don't like being teased.

Bully: Yeah, you said that already, parrot. So what. You're still an idiot. (Bully walks away.)

The Broken Record Technique is effective for children and adults because it simply restates the person's position. There is simply no way for another person (the aggressor) to get his or her way.

Broadly stated, assertiveness training involves teaching children the social skills they need to effectively deal with others, to fulfill their needs and to stick up for their rights. Assertiveness training relies on several behavioral principles, including being reinforced for new learned assertive behaviors, becoming desensitized towards negative stimuli (i.e., outside stimuli like teasing, bullying, and peer pressure, as well as internal emotional states like anxiety and fear), and learning the principle of non-reinforcement by ignoring.

Two behavioral skills that are particularly important to many children with poor social skills are Practicing Criticism and Giving a Compliment. Children in therapy or counseling typically have a poor self-concept related to their problems. Even children who seem defiant and arrogant may suffer from feelings of inadequacy, and their behavior may be in part a reaction to statements that reinforce their poor self-image.

Teaching children to accept criticism will help them learn more appropriate ways to respond to negative comments. The therapist or counselor will begin by having the child describe a variety of situations where he or she feels criticized. It is not important whether the child feels that the criticism is justified or not; it is only important that the child learn to respond in ways which do not make him feel devalued and do not devalue others.

Next, the therapist should role-play at least five scenarios with the child, having the child practice accepting criticism, while also practicing specific assertive behaviors. The following is a list of specific behaviors that the child can practice in his or her role-playing:

> **Acknowledging the criticism**: "I know I shouldn't have shoved Tommy in line." (using a firm tone of voice)

> **Stating feelings:** "I was angry when Tommy said I was ugly." (making eye contact with the person giving the criticism; having

a "positive" body posture)

Asserting one's rights: "I know I was wrong to shove Tommy, but he shouldn't make fun of me."

Correcting examples of stereotyping or prejudice: "It is wrong to make fun of someone because of his appearance."

The majority of children who have behavioral problems respond to criticism or negative reinforcement in ways that make things worse. Teaching children to respond appropriately to criticism is an important way to break a chain of self-defeating behavior.

The other side of the coin of learning to deal with negative reinforcement is learning to provide positive reinforcement to others. Teaching children to give compliments may seem like an odd behavioral program, yet it is a form of assertive behavior that leads to social acceptance and approval.

The therapist would begin by teaching the child the general principles of positive reinforcement and their value. The therapist should emphasize that a compliment is a type of positive reinforcement only when it is sincere and meaningful to the other person (e.g., saying that someone "looks nice" when she doesn't would not be taken as a compliment). Some children will then need to practice identifying things for which to compliment a person. Generally, people like to receive compliments for what they are already proud of, and the child can be taught to identify the ways that people call attention to themselves or their achievements. The child can practice giving compliments to the therapist or other people whom the therapist feels comfortable in bringing into the office. Ideally, the therapist could videotape the child giving compliments and then have him rate himself on the list below.

How to Give a Compliment

Check the behaviors you observe:

—Makes eye contact
—Speaks clearly

—Identifies an appropriate thing to compliment
—Gives a compliment at an appropriate time
—Personalizes the compliment (e.g., I like your new sneakers. I saw them on TV and they look cool.)
—Follows up the compliment with an expression of interest
(You really ran fast in the relay races yesterday. Do you play on the soccer team?)

Giving sincere compliments (positive reinforcement) is an important social skill to learn and may be particularly valuable for children who are normally seen as "difficult" to help them develop friendships with their peers as well as closer relationships with adults.

The Special Role of Karate in Helping Children
#52. Selecting the Right "Master"
#53. Using Karate for Nonviolence

Theory: *Eastern Philosophy; Humanistic Psychology*

For many years, counselors and therapists have recommended karate or other martial arts for specific children. Although I have only dealt with a few cases in which I recommended karate for an emotionally troubled child, this intervention did not seem to be particularly helpful in spite of the fact that it seemed like it would have important benefits for specific children.

While lecturing on short-term therapy techniques around the country, I have asked my audiences if anyone has used this technique successfully, and I always have three or four people who offer inspiring stories of how martial arts training has helped children. The most common group of children with which this technique seems to be used are children who have been abused or otherwise "victimized." Therapists report that even withdrawn and inhibited boys and girls seem to respond to martial arts training conducted by a sensitive and thoughtful instructor.

A second group of children that seems to be helped by this technique is overly aggressive children, particularly over the age of 10. The benefit of teaching martial arts to this group is of course the nonviolent philosophy at the core of martial arts training. Aggressive children under the age of 10 may have a difficult time understanding the paradoxes inherent in this training. Whatever they are told about the "peaceful nature" of martial arts training becomes overshadowed by the endless karate fights that they see on TV and in the movies, and it is difficult for them to focus on the paradoxical message of how learning about how to fight can be a road to peace.

The critical element of whether or not this technique can be used successfully as an adjunct to therapy is clearly in the character and philosophy of the martial arts teacher. Karate schools are a business, and, like any other business, they need customers. Like it or not, many instructors will tell the therapist or counselor what they want to hear instead of what really happens at the karate school.

To really make karate into a therapeutic tool, it will be necessary for the therapist to develop a therapeutic alliance with the instructor, just as he or she would develop an alliance with a family member or schoolteacher who would be involved in the child's therapy. The karate instructor will then be functioning as a cotherapist and should obviously have the same goals, values, and interest in the child as any other cotherapist would.

In evaluating the appropriateness of a particular instructor of a martial arts school, the therapist should inquire as to how the philosophy of the martial art is taught and integrated into the athletic training. Eastern Philosophy can have a significant effect on a young person's life, particularly when other forces in the child's life might be influencing him or her towards self-destructive behaviors.

Dr. Terrence Webster-Doyle and Atrium Press have been eloquent leaders of the movement to combine principles of education, psychology, and the martial arts to teach young people to resolve conflict peacefully. A psychologist and educator, Dr. Webster-Doyle has written many books for children to help them understand karate as a way to teach relationship-building skills and nonviolence. *The Eye of the Hurricane* (Atrium Society, 1992), for example, contains a collection of stories and parables that demonstrate the basic principles of karate. One story called "The Empty Cup" describes how two great and wise Martial Arts Masters were visited by a university professor. The professor had studied for many years to understand the essence of karate, but she still did not understand the meaning of karate, the Empty

Self, and how it could bring peace. The older Master poured his guest some tea as she spoke, and kept pouring it even when the cup was full! Finally, the professor could stand it no longer and exclaimed, "The cup is full. No more will go in!"

"Like this cup," the Master explained, "your mind is full of questions and seeking answers! Until you empty your cup, no more can go in. Likewise, until you empty your mind, you cannot receive anything."

Books like Dr. Webster-Doyle's *Martial Arts Guide for Parents: Helping Your Child Resolve Conflicts Peacefully* (Weatherhill Press, 1999) can aid you in helping children find the therapeutic benefit in martial arts training.

Teaching Altruism: Getting Kids to Be Better or Getting Better Kids?
#54. An Act of Kindness Every Day
#55. Giving Children Assignments to Help Others

Theory: *Humanistic Psychology*

There are many reasons children misbehave, but there are relatively few ways that we deal with their misbehavior. Most therapists will advocate an effective discipline strategy along with a program for rewarding positive behavior.

In many cases, however, the frequency of misbehavior far outweighs the positive behavior, and so the program quickly degenerates into a power struggle between the adult and the child. Additionally, behavioral programs are typically not fun to implement, and unfortunately many parents give up on them too soon because there is not enough positive reinforcement for the child or the adult.

To help diffuse this battle over misbehavior, I often recommend that parents consider building positive behaviors rather than just concentrating on the negative ones. Too often, parents are so concerned with the day-to-day tantrums, aggression, or general willfulness of their child that they forget the important altruistic behaviors that may be missing from the child's repertoire, including helpfulness, sharing, kindness, and charity.

Instead of recommending a simple behavioral or discipline program to parents, I have on many occasions recommended a "Good Kid" Program, which combines a behavioral program with a systematic program of teaching children positive altruistic behaviors.

Good acts are really much more important than not acting badly. Where learning to misbehave less frequently may build self-control, learning to act in ways that help other people builds self-control and self-esteem.

When children learn helping behaviors, they learn to connect to the world in a positive way; they feel like they belong.

The book *Random Acts of Kindness* was published by the editors of Conari Press as a collection of stories about simple things that people do for each other that can have lifelong effects. This book has started a movement of people interested in the inherent goodness in all of us and how easily it can be expressed.

Kids' Random Acts of Kindness (Conari Press, 1994) is a collection of letters that children wrote to the publisher after hearing about the original book. The letters range from sweet to bittersweet, and all reveal the struggle of children to let go of their egocentrism and develop empathy for others.

Dr. Dawna Markova writes in the introduction, "What can we do (for our children) that will foster their open-hearted hopefulness, engage their need to collaborate, be an incentive to utilize their natural competency and compassion? What if instead of condemning the darkness, we turn our children towards the light by giving them something to move towards? What if we show them ways to connect, reach out, weave themselves into the web of relationships that is called community? What if we helped children expand their repertoire by offering them new possibilities for forward movement so that they could learn to translate their anger, rebellion, defiance into an active challenge they could be proud of?"

Teaching children positive, even altruistic behavior, is such an obvious antidote to misbehavior that I sometimes wonder why therapists and counselors don't prescribe it more often. But I know the answer to this question. We live in a society that tends to isolate us as individuals, and psychotherapy, for all its merits, tends to do the same by focusing on the individual rather than on the individual within the context of society. But all children can benefit from turning outward towards the world, learning that "by helping others, we help ourselves."

Asking children to do one kind thing every day is a simple request. They can:

- Hold the door open for someone.

- Wish someone well who is ill.

- Send a card to someone who is lonely

- Put a quarter in a charity jar at the local convenience store.

- Help younger siblings with homework.

- Take out the trash, even though it is not their turn.

Being kinder can be a family project. Every day at dinner, each family member could report what they had done for someone else. What could be more important or helpful to a child?

With children who have severe social problems–including aggressiveness and defiance–I recommend making more of a concentrated effort to teach them altruistic behavior. *The Helping Hands Handbook* (Random House, 1991) describes over 100 projects that children are currently doing to help others, from celebrating the birthdays of people in nursing homes, to adopting a whale, to being a secret pal to a teacher and making him or her feel more appreciated. For older children, I recommend *The Kid's Guide to Social Action* by Barbara A. Lewis (Free Spirit Publishing, 1991), which contains step-by-step guides to help children change the world with letter-writing campaigns, fund-raising, petitions, and much more.

The next time you recommend a discipline program or a behavioral program to a parent, think about helping them implement a "Good Kid" Program as well. It could be your "random act of kindness."

Teaching Children The Nonverbal Language of Social Skills
#56. Observing Nonverbal Language
#57. Feelings Charades
#58. Dictionary of Facial Expressions
#59. Audio Dictionary
#60. Walk the Plank: A Game about Interpersonal Space

Theory: *Learning Theory, Developmental*

Drs. Stephen Nowicki, Jr. and Marshall Duke, in their book *Helping the Child Who Doesn't Fit In* (Peachtree Publishers, 1992), refer to children who have difficulty in getting along because of their inability to read nonverbal cues as "dyssemic." Comparing this problem to a language disorder, they explain that dyssemic children do not effectively interpret and understand the nonverbal language of others, including facial expressions, personal space, body language, posture, and voice tone. The authors hypothesize that many children who are rejected by their peers may be having social difficulties because of this unrecognized problem.

Many diagnostic categories have associated social problems, including children with attention deficit disorders, conduct disorders, depression, and so on. Many children with learning disabilities or developmental delays also have associated problems in reading nonverbal and social cues. In truth, there are relatively few children who come in for therapy who do not have some problems in the way they relate to others, which frequently includes a misinterpretation or distortion of nonverbal behavior.

Ironically, children often respond more readily to learning nonverbal social cues than learning verbal social behavior. Learning to read and interpret nonverbal signals is like learning a secret language–one which very few people know.

Nowicki and Duke suggest that one of the first steps in teaching children to understand the nonverbal behavior of others is to learn to observe it. This is easily accomplished by having children watch videotaped TV shows or movies with the sound turned off. The "trainer" (therapist, teacher, or even parent) could then "freeze" the action at certain points and ask the child to describe how the people on the screen are feeling, paying attention exclusively to their nonverbal cues (posture, body distance, expression, and so on).

The authors also suggest a variety of practical exercises to help children identify and understand nonverbal social cues.

Feelings Charades is a fun and easy game to play with a small group of children. Simply make a list of common feelings words and put them in a bowl. Starting with the youngest player, each child in turn must select a word from the bowl and then act out that word until one of the other players guesses the feeling. In each round, the player who guesses the correct feeling and the one who acts it out each get a point. The person who has the most points at the end of the allotted time is the winner. After each round, the adult facilitator can ask questions about how we look and what we do that shows our feelings.

Two other interesting activities that can help children be more aware of nonverbal social language are making a Dictionary of Facial Expressions and an Audio Dictionary of Voice Tones. You can use the following list of feelings for both dictionaries, making it shorter for younger children and expanding it for older children.

To make a Dictionary of Facial Expressions, just write each feeling on the top of a piece of paper and then have the child find magazine pictures or photographs that depict each feeling to paste on that page. During the activity, you will have a chance to talk about the way we "read" facial expressions, as facial expressions can often speak much louder than words. Having a mirror nearby will allow the child to practice making his own different facial expressions. Older children (above the age of nine) can learn that the way their facial expressions are perceived can be an important factor in how they are treated by other people.

Feelings Words

affectionate	afraid
anxious	brave
bored	confused
disappointed	dreamy
embarrassed	excited
greedy	guilty
happy	interested
irritable	jealous
lonely	loving
mad	peaceful
pleased	proud
sad	satisfied
scared	shocked
shy	sick
silly	smart
stressed	surprised
thoughtful	tired
upset	worried

To make an Audio Dictionary of Voice Tones, simply have the child say a sentence using each feeling word and record it with a tape recorder. The child should be instructed to use a voice tone that reflects the feeling in each sentence.

The next step in making an audio dictionary is to make a recording of other people's voice tones. The therapist can ask important people in the child's life (i.e., father, mother, teacher, etc.) to record each of the feelings words in a sentence using the appropriate voice tone. This will help the child be sensitive to the nuances of voice tone that each person has and will also sensitize the other people in the child's life to this issue.

There are many games that can be played with children to help them be more aware of their body movement, body control, and personal space. One game described to me recently at a workshop is called Walk the Plank. The therapist takes masking tape and measures out two parallel strips of tape on the floor, about three feet apart and six feet in length. All the players are told to stand between the two pieces of tape (the plank).

Then the players are instructed to get in order by height and walk off the plank. Naturally, no one can step outside the lines, or they will fall into the water. This game forces children to be very aware of their bodies so as not to fall off the plank or push anyone off either!

For other physical games that stress cooperation rather than competition, see *New Games* and *New Games for the Whole Family* by Dale N. LeFevre (Putnam Publishing, 1988) and *Playfair: Everybody's Guide to Noncompetitive Play* by Matt Weinstein and Joel Goodman (Impact Publishers, 1980).

#61. Time on Your Hands: Teaching Children to Be on Time

Theory: *Behavior Modification*

A characteristic of dyssemic children, as well as children with ADD, is their difficulty in time estimation. Requests for these children to be at the dinner table at 6:15 p.m. or to be in their seat promptly at 9:00 a.m. are typically taken as reasonable enough by the child, yet these children never seem to be in the right place at the right time.

I invented the game I call "Time on Your Hands" for a very good-natured ADD child who was driving his parents and teacher crazy because of his lateness. I have always liked this game because it solves the problem immediately; you can't win, or even play the game, unless you are on time. To play, a child will need a simple digital wristwatch, and he or she must know how to read it, at least in a limited way. The therapist or parent must identify the exact times that the child needs to punctually be at a certain place. Typically, these include all meals, when class begins in the morning and after recess, when it is time to do homework, and when it is time to get ready for bed.

The parent then draws a picture of how a digital watch should look at each of these important times:

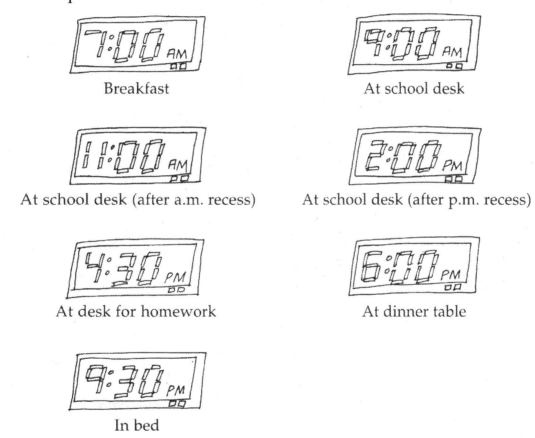

Breakfast   At school desk

At school desk (after a.m. recess)   At school desk (after p.m. recess)

At desk for homework   At dinner table

In bed

Next the parent and teacher tape a picture of the watch with the correct time at the location where the child is supposed to be at that time. For example, the picture of the watch at 7:00 a.m. is taped to the breakfast table, the pictures of the watch at 9:00 a.m., 11:00 a.m. and 2:00 p.m. are taped to the child's desk, and so on.

The game is played very simply: The child has to hold his wristwatch next to each picture of the correct time so that the numbers match up exactly.

Each time his watch matches the picture, he gets a point.

In other words, at breakfast he must match his watch to the picture of the watch at 7:00 a.m.; at school, he must match his watch to the picture of the watch at 9:00 a.m.; and so on. Every time he matches the picture, the child gets a point, and he can cash in the points at the end of the week for prizes or special activities.

This game is easy to play and fun for children, but it does require an adult to be at the right location throughout the day, which can be difficult. For this reason, I recommend that "Time on Your Hands" be played on a limited basis: three consecutive days, and then just one day a week for a month (i.e., every Tuesday). On the other days, random reinforcement can be given (i.e., a point) when the adult sees the child in place at the right time.

Parenting Techniques

Most therapists and counselors who work with children in private practice will tell you they spend as much time working with parents as they do with children. Professionals who work in schools or other institutional settings will have less contact with parents, and they will depend on parents (or other caretakers) to implement or assist in important parts of the therapeutic plan.

Whatever your work setting, there is no denying that parents know the child better and have more influence on the child than any professional ever will. To the extent that you can engage the parents as "cotherapists" and motivate them to be instruments of change, the better the prognosis will be for any child.

#62. Getting the Parents to Be Your Allies: The Menu of Techniques

Theory: *Multimodal Therapy*

There are many techniques that can be recommended to parents which will support and supplement a child's counseling sessions. But therapists frequently have a difficult time in eliciting the cooperation of the parents or other family members. The parents may express their conscious concern and faith in the therapeutic methods, but on an unconscious level, for a variety of reasons, parents may work to undo the therapist's work.

Every effort should be made to ally oneself with the parents from the onset of therapy. Some therapists will have parents observe the sessions from behind a one-way mirror so that the parents don't feel displaced. Other therapists take time at the end of the session to bring the parents in and give them an update on the child's progress, often assigning specific therapeutic "homework" for the week. Generally speaking, the more parents feel involved in the therapy from the initial session, the more they are likely to ally themselves with the therapist.

Dr. John March, Director of Duke University's program for Mental Illness and Anxiety Disorders, uses a multimodal treatment approach in working with children with Obsessive Compulsive Disorders (OCD) and works diligently to "empower" the parents as cotherapists. In his short-term therapy approach, Dr. March realizes that it is the parents who will spend the most time with the child, and they will ultimately be the ones who will effect a reduction in the child's OCD symptoms. It is therefore reasonable that they should assist in choosing the techniques that will help the child change, even helping to choose the correct combination of medications.

Dr. March's approach combines a group of medications (serotonin reuptake inhibitors) with very specific forms of cognitive therapy and behavior modification. But Dr. March notes that it is not clear from the empirical research exactly which medications or combinations of medications will be effective with any given child. So he and his associates outline a "Chinese menu" to the parents, giving the pluses and minuses of the different medications. Naturally, they rule out certain medications that would be contraindicated (e.g., a child with an abnormal EKG isn't a candidate for clomipramine), and the team also suggests which combination of drugs might work the best.

Letting parents assist in choosing methods to help their children is in itself a technique. To make the choice, parents must obviously learn about the various possible techniques, discussing them from an objective "scientific" viewpoint. This makes the parents much more open to learning about the technique, because they are being treated like responsible, intelligent adults instead of being "taught" to be better parents.

Additionally, giving the parents a menu of techniques and asking for their input emphasizes that at least part of the responsibility for the success of the treatment rests with them. This is particularly important when discussing a change in behavioral management and discipline techniques—a common recommendation of therapists and counselors.

There are many different approaches that a parent should be made aware of, as well as the fact that some work much more quickly than others. In choosing from a menu of behavioral techniques, the therapist should guide the parent in choosing techniques that are consistent with their needs as well as the child's. Some techniques require a significant amount of time, while others do not. Some techniques require more of a confrontative approach, and others are more accepting of the child.

Generally speaking, the more confrontative techniques, such as the Overcorrection Technique (#71) work more quickly, but no technique will work unless it is consistent with the parents' philosophy and ability. (Note: To learn more about Dr. March's treatment of children with OCD, read *How I Ran OCD Off My Land: A Guide to the Cognitive Behavioral Treatment of Obsessive Compulsive Disorders in Children*. Write Dr. John March, Duke University Medical Center, Suite 3527, Durham, NC 27710).

#63. Targeting Behavior

Theory: *Behavior Modification*

Many times parents come to a therapist or counselor with a multitude of complaints about a child: "She doesnt try in school, she never helps around the house, she ties up the phone, she doesn't listen to her father," and so on.

When this happens, I explain to the parents that their child may have many problems that need attention, but it is more effective if we work on one problem at a time. To help the parent determine the most significant problem, I give them a picture of a target and ask them to write all the problems around the target, with the most unimportant problems on the outside, the next most important in the next ring, and so on until the most important behavior is in the bull's-eye of the target.

The behavior in the bull's-eye is naturally the behavior that we work on first. The target is also an important metaphor for finding the best ways to address the most important behavior. How do you make it more likely that you will hit the bull's-eye? (Stand closer to the target, or, in other words, spend more time with the child.) What if you miss the bull's-eye? (You may still hit some other area of the target, or, in other words, you may still be able to affect some other area of the problem.) How do you hit the bull's-eye more frequently? (Practice!)

Use the target to focus parents on the most important problems.

#64. Putting Parents on a Behavior Program

Theory: *Behavior Modification*

Everyone is sometimes frustrated in their effort to help children with problems, particularly children who have severe behavioral manifestations. It is the therapist's job to find techniques that can be supported by the parents in ways that are consistent with their values, style, and psychological strengths. But even so, parents may get frustrated with their child's difficulty in changing and, unfortunately, may become less motivated to carry out the program correctly and consistently.

I like to emphasize to parents how hard it is for anyone to change, and I ask them about the times when they have had to change a behavior (almost everyone has tried to lose weight, stop smoking, or overcome a bad habit). It is important to help parents see both their successes and their failures in order for them to understand the basic principles of behavior modification, including the power of reinforcers, dispositional factors, the role of biochemistry, and so on.

After this discussion, I help the parent to relate the child's problem and its amenability to change to something that they have had to change: "Is it as hard for your son as losing weight is for you?," "Is it easier for your daughter to face her fear of dogs than for you to face your fear of flying?" In most cases, the parent has some behavior that he or she wants to change that is equivalent to the child's problem.

I then ask the parent if he or she would like me to design a behavioral program for him or her, just as I did for the child. Some parents decline but become more motivated to help their child and try harder to confront the issues of consistency and patience in getting behavioral change. Other parents agree, and this gives me the opportunity to teach them more about the behavioral principles that can help them change as well.

#65. Using Mnemonics to Help Parents Carry Out Effective Discipline Techniques

Theory: *Learning Theory*

There are many reasons why even motivated parents have difficulty in carrying out a therapist's instructions or suggestions. In most cases, we are asking them to do something other than "what comes naturally." Whatever techniques we suggest take time and energy, a scarce commodity in most households. But we can make many techniques easier for parents to use by giving them simple mnemonics, or memory aids, to help them remember the principles they need to apply.

For example, there are two mnemonics associated with using the time-out technique effectively:

- The child should be in time-out for one minute for each year of their age (not to exceed 10 minutes).

- The "6/60" rule is that parents should not say more than six words to the child when placing him in time-out, and should have the child in the corner within 60 seconds (thus keeping opportunities to engage and distract the parent at a minimum).

Then there is the 4:1 principle for giving children positive verbal reinforcement:

- For every one negative thing that you hear yourself saying to a child, say four positive things.

This type of mnemonic condenses the technique into its primary components and makes the principles very concrete and easier to follow.

Getting People to Cooperate in the Therapy by Giving Them No Other Choice
#66. Double-Binds
#67. Forced Choices

Theory: *Strategic Family Therapy*

A more confrontative, but also a more effective, approach to getting parents to cooperate in their child's therapeutic program is to put them in a "double-bind." A double-bind gives the parents (or the child) only two choices, but either choice will move the child and the child's system in the right therapeutic direction. For example:

- A defiant and aggressive child refused to cooperate in the behavioral program designed for him. He was given the choice of either participating in the program or attending a military school. (He chose to participate in the behavioral program.)

- A husband and wife going through a separation continued to have both physical and verbal fights. The court required the family to go through 10 hours of therapy before the custody hearing. The therapist gave the couple a choice of either making quick progress on resolving their conflicts in couples therapy or working on them with the child present. The therapist explained that if the child was destined to have "mule-headed" and "aggressive" parents, then there was no sense in hiding it from her. (The parents chose to protect their child from their arguing and entered couples' therapy with a more conciliatory attitude.)

- An eleven-year-old girl refused to accept the therapist's request to play a therapeutic game. The girl could either play the game with the therapist or watch him play the game by himself. (She eventually played the game.)

- A mother felt overwhelmed by her parenting responsibilities as she tried to hold down a job and recover from a drug and alcohol problem. Her son was becoming truant and failing his classes. The mother was given the choice of going into counseling for herself or having her own mother move into her house and run the household. (She chose to have her mother move in, who then restored order to the household.)

The critical element in creating a double-bind choice in therapy is that both choices must be agreed upon by all parties, but one choice must be less desirable, although it will reach the therapeutic goal. As you can see from the above examples, this can involve difficult choices, and the more difficult the choice, the more the therapist must be convinced that the parents or child are committed to both alternative directions.

For instance, in the first example, the parents must initially agree to send their child to military school if he refuses to participate in the behavioral program. But that is only the first step. The parents must also agree to investigate various schools, get applications, explore how they will pay for the school, and so on. The parents must treat this as a real alternative or the child may simply see it as an idle threat.

In forcing the parents into difficult choices, the therapist may feel like he or she is in a judgmental position rather than taking a neutral therapeutic stance. This is in fact the case, but it may be the only way to insure therapeutic progress, and if the parents cannot accept that hard choices must be made, then they may not be amenable to therapy.

Creating Forced Choices is a technique that can be used with teachers as well as parents. Therapists should recognize that teachers often assume a parenting as well as an educational role with their students but may have a great deal of ambivalence about this position.

On many occasions, a counselor or other school staff member has described to me how well-meaning teachers undermine their efforts by dismissing ideas off-handedly:

> "Oh, I've tried that before; it won't work."

> "That's much too much trouble. I have 30 other children in the class as well, you know."

> "John's parents aren't going to like that."

The counselor can avoid going back and forth trying to provide an acceptable technique by giving the resistant teacher (or childcare worker or parent) a list of techniques that could be tried. The list of techniques will ideally include the pros and cons of each technique. It is then up to the teacher to decide which technique(s) to choose or to offer a new technique of her own. In giving the teacher a forced choice, the counselor puts herself in the role of an "expert resource," and the teacher is given the power to choose which technique she sees as the best, putting her in the role of "expert facilitator.," This type of forced choice puts adversaries on the same side, working together towards the common therapeutic goal.

#68. Positive Direction

Theory: *Behavior Modification*

A very simple parenting technique that can be taught in just a few minutes is called Positive Direction, suggested by Drs. Sam and Michael Goldstein as a particularly effective technique for children with attention deficit disorders (in *Managing Attention Disorders in Children*, John Wiley and Sons, Inc., 1990). Research suggests that parents who use positive directions often achieve greater compliance than those who use negative directions. Negative directions tell the child what not to do:

> *Don't make noises at the table. It's disgusting.*

> *Don't hit your sister. What's the matter with you?*

> *Shut up! You're giving me a headache!*

Positive directions guide the child towards more appropriate alternatives to their maladaptive or unruly behaviors and, more importantly, do not demean the child:

> *Making noises at the table disturbs people during dinner. If you need to make noises, you can excuse yourself from the table and go outside for five minutes.*

> *When you hit your sister you will have to go to time-out. Try hitting this pillow when you are angry.*

> *I have a headache, and noise makes it worse. Would you please go upstairs and play with your Legos for one half hour? I'll check on you at 4:30.*

Changing negative directions into positive ones can easily be taught to parents. Have them write down the things that they typically say to their children in one column, and then, in a second column, change those statements into directions to the child that tell him, very specifically, what he should be doing instead.

This technique can also be used to help teachers who may be overly critical or harsh with children but still need immediate compliance.

#69. Preventing the Problem

Theory: *Behavior Modification*

Many of the behavior modification programs used with children focus on changing the consequences of unwanted behaviors–increasing positive reinforcement for appropriate behaviors and negative reinforcement for maladaptive or dysfunctional behaviors. But it is just as important and effective to change the antecedents of unwanted behavior: in other words, to reduce the chance of the inappropriate behavior occurring by changing the original stimulus.

Drs. Sam and Michael Goldstein (*Managing Attention Disorders in Children: A Guide for Practitioners,* John Wiley and Sons, 1990) broaden this behavioral concept in what they refer to as Preventive Intervention. They suggest two ways to prevent a specific behavior from occurring: educating the child and changing the environment.

Educating the child can range from short and direct explanations to signs placed around the house (e.g., sign on the child's door: "Pick up your clothes before you go to bed," or sign on the child's book bag: "Don't forget to bring your homework to class.") Changing the environment could range from locking up toys and unplugging the TV when a child is supposed to be doing homework to pairing the child with a study partner at school to provide him with a good role model.

Although Preventive Intervention may seem somewhat mundane and obvious as a technique, it can be a powerful tool when used consistently by all adults involved in the therapeutic plan. The chart on the next page may be useful in planning Preventive Intervention.

Preventive Intervention Chart

Name of child:_____

Filled out by:_____

Date:_____

INAPPROPRIATE BEHAVIOR	WAYS TO EDUCATE CHILD	WAYS TO CHANGE ENVIRONMENT
1.		
2.		
3.		
4.		
5.		

#70. The Good Behavior Book

Theory: *Values Clarification, Behavior Modification*

A technique closely related to Preventive Intervention involves asking the child to keep a Good Behavior Book. The Good Behavior Book is a type of diary where the child (or the child's parents or teachers) record all incidents of good behavior each day. Good behavior should be broadly defined to include not only specific behavioral goals, such as on a behavioral chart, but also behaviors such as helping, sharing, good manners, and so on. The Good Behavior Book can be more like a scrapbook, including pictures, tests or papers with good grades, drawings, etc.

In using a Good Behavior Book with a child, you will be simultaneously using a number of important psychological principles from at least four psychotherapeutic disciplines, including:

- Rewarding positive behaviors and ignoring negative behaviors. (Behavioral Therapy)

- Spending time and energy to help the child understand how much you value good behavior. (Client-Centered Therapy)

- Documenting success. (Behavioral Therapy)

- Bringing the child together with powerful role models. For example, someone very important to the child might be chosen to help him or her with his or her Good Behavior Book. The positive nature of the technique virtually insures that the inter-action of the adult and child will be positive. (Strategic Family Therapy)

- Providing an opportunity for an adult to direct the child towards increasing his good behaviors. (Cognitive Therapy)

#71. The Overcorrection Technique

Theory: *Behavior Modification*

The Overcorrection Technique is an underused parenting technique that can be extremely effective in the right circumstances. It is a behavioral technique originally introduced by Azrin and Foxx in toilet training intellectually impaired children and was later applied by Azrin and Nunn to a variety of dysfunctional habits (*Habit Control in a Day*, Pocket Books, 1977). Unlike other techniques that rely on negatively reinforcing a given behavior, this technique requires that the child actually perform and put into practice the appropriate behavior.

This stage of the technique, called positive practice, assumes that the child must learn to substitute a new behavior for the old dysfunctional one, and that following the laws of behavior modification, the new behavior must be practiced many times before it can be learned.

Take, for example, the child who comes home from school, brushes past his mother with barely a "hello," throws his book bag and coat on the floor, and stretches out on the couch to watch TV instead of going upstairs to do his homework. The positive practice for this child would be to come in and greet his mother respectfully, put away his things, and go upstairs to his room and start his homework. This child would not just have to do this once, but perhaps 10 times, as a consequence of his original rude and slovenly behavior. Whenever he came home from school and did not act appropriately, he would have to do the positive practice procedure 10 times. If he refused, his mother would have to physically guide him through this procedure. If he resisted, he would have to go to time-out or get some other negative consequence until he agreed to do the positive practice.

The second stage of the Overcorrection Procedure is called the restitution phase, and it is equally important to practicing the positive behavior. It is assumed that the child's original misbehavior has hurt or at least inconvenienced someone, and the child must now make restitution. In the above example, perhaps the boy would have to wash his mother's car or do some extra chore. In providing restitution, the child is required to "make things right," making his mother feel better about what happened and presumably making him feel better about himself, since he has now evened the score and done something that can be appreciated.

The Overcorrection Procedure can be a difficult one for parents to implement. It isn't fun. But on the other hand, when it is used correctly and consistently, it can result in a rapid change of even very entrenched behaviors.

#72. Turning Off the TV–The Most Powerful Behavioral Tool (That Nobody Uses)

Theory: *Behavior Modification*

When I lecture about choosing different techniques in short-term therapy, I like to make the point that techniques should be seen on a continuum of "power and intrusion." Certain techniques are simply more powerful than others in effecting quick change; but unfortunately, in almost all cases, the more powerful the technique, the more intrusive or disruptive it is to the child's life (see *Short-Term Therapy with Children*, Shapiro, Childswork/Childsplay, LLC, 1994). In giving examples of how behavioral techniques fit on this continuum, I end my explanation by talking about the most powerful, intrusive and horrendous thing you can do to an American child: taking away the TV.

When we consider any behavior modification program, we must also consider the motivating strength of the positive and negative reinforcers that underlie the program. For better or worse, the TV (and I include videotapes and video games as well as regular TV) has a tremendous value to almost all children in this country. It would be difficult to overestimate the power of TV on a family. Most parents know that TV is not a good thing for children, and yet the average American child watches a mind-numbing 24 hours of TV a week! We can ask ourselves: "How can parents let this happen? How can parents let children do something which is so obviously bad for them?" But the answer is equally obvious: TV viewing time is a very difficult thing to control in a family.

For this same reason, therapists and counselors rarely recommend taking the TV away as a discipline technique. Although this may work as a way to get children to behave, parents rarely feel that they can consistently control the family's TV habits. One of the few things that can help is a gadget called TV Allowance. Manufactured by MindMaster, Inc. (7400 Red Road, Suite 21, South Miami, FL, 33143; (800) 231-4410), TV Allowance is a device that plugs in between the TV and the electrical socket and allows the parent to program in the number of hours that children can use the TV. To turn on the TV, children have to enter their own four-digit code, which then automatically starts debiting the allocated minutes from their TV account. When a child's time is used up during a given week, the TV simply shuts off.

TV Allowance is one of the few ways that parents can really take control of the TV. For the purpose of behavior modification, TV time can be integrated into a token economy system, where children can earn additional TV time by meeting their behavioral goals and lose time when they have misbehaved. Naturally, to make this program work, children cannot have access to other TVs, including those at friends' houses.

Controlling TV-watching can be a challenging task, but it can have a major impact on a child's life. Not only does the adult now control a very powerful force, but think of all the healthy and productive things children can do when they are not watching TV!

#73. Stress Inoculation

Theory: *Behavior Therapy; Stress Management*

Often, parents seek the advice of a therapist or a counselor in anticipation of their child's reaction to an upcoming problem or event. Frequently they are concerned about how a child will react to hearing about their separation or divorce. Or perhaps they are worried about how their child will react to an anticipated death of a grandparent, a family move, or a hospitalization.

Dr. Archibald D. Hart explains in his book *Stress and Your Child* (Word Publishers, 1992) that children can be "inoculated" against potentially overwhelming stress by exposure to small amounts of stress in anticipation of a problem, much the way that we inoculate a child against an infectious disease by injecting him or her with a mild version of the disease organism. Dr. Hart explains: "When we inoculate our children against stress, we expose them gradually, under controlled conditions, to more and more stress, while at the same time showing them how to cope with stress. Over time, this process helps to build strength of character, a healthier and more positive outlook, a sense of personal competence and a willingness to take on challenges and not to avoid risks."

Dr. Hart suggests a five-step process in preparing children to deal with stress:

1. Gradually expose children to problems.

   • Avoid overprotecting children.

   • Tell children the truth about family problems in simplified and age-appropriate ways.

   • Let children know that there are real problems in the world, allowing them to help those in need.

   • Give children responsibilities that will challenge their resourcefulness.

2. Resist the urge to rescue children.

   • Allow children to solve their own problems–first simple ones, then more complex ones.

   • Allow children to experience the "negative" emotions that accompany problems (e.g., don't immediately replace a lost or deceased pet to keep a child from being sad).

3. Teach healthy "self-talk."

   • Encourage children to say things to themselves that are rational, self-encouraging, optimistic, etc.

4. Teach children to allow themselves adequate time for recovery from periods of overstress.

   • Many children feel a letdown after a big event like a test, a school play, a big football game, etc. Dr. Hart refers to this as "post-adrenaline depression." This is a natural part of the human condition and is a way that our body tells us to take a rest and recover after a period of great stress and exertion. This is a normal occurrence of which children should be aware. Learning to allow time to recover from stress will have lifelong effects in terms of building good coping skills.

5. Teach children to filter stressors.
- Children can learn to control their emotional reactions to specific events: "Is this a test worth worrying about?"; "Is it really important that I wasn't invited to Gary's party?" Humans have a reflexive stress response to fears of danger, loss, and security. Often this response will generalize to less significant events. Children can learn to control inappropriate emotional reactions to stressors that are less important through a variety of stress-reduction techniques.

#74. Family Rules Served Up at Solution Meals

Theory: *Family Therapy*

As you know by now from reading this book, I like to approach problems from a playful perspective if at all possible. That's why instead of simply asking parents to initiate family meetings once a week in order to go over family rules and issues, I encourage them to have a Solution Meal.

A Solution Meal is a designated weekly meal, perhaps a Sunday dinner, where the family discusses problems that have come up in the previous week and solutions that can be implemented during the next week. The meal itself should be made as enjoyable as possible, perhaps with favorite dishes or a special cake to celebrate the family. But the real solutions come when the food is eaten...literally. Before coming to the dinner, each person writes down something that he or she can do to contribute to the family during the next week. For example:

I am going to help Mary study for her spelling test.

I am going to wash Dad's car.

I am going to rake the leaves.

I am going to come home from work early and take everyone out to McDonald's.

These "solutions" to having a happier family are placed under another family member's plate. If the family has clear glass plates, the solution will be revealed when the dinner is eaten. Otherwise, the solutions should be read by each person when the dinner plates are cleared. Most importantly, each member of the family should commit him- or herself to making a positive contribution to the family as a whole, or by helping a specific family member.

#75. Family Cooperative Games

Theory: *Values Clarification*

Cooperative games are very different from the competitive games that most families play Instead of one person winning and everyone else losing, either everyone wins or everyone loses. The cooperative game movement has been led by a company called Family Pastimes in Perth, Ontario, Canada, [(613) 267-4819], which for more than 20 years has been making games based on this principle.

One of my favorites is called "Mountaineering." In this game, players work together to scale a mountain peak. If they work together, they reach the top, but if they don't cooperate, nobody can get down!

There are also many family cooperative games that you can make. One of my favorites is an adaptation of a game invented by Jim Deacove (the founder of Family Pastimes and inventor of the company's games). The original game was a type of hockey game, using air-pump bulbs to blow a small cork ball around a wooden board. The game was great fun to play, and players were forced to cooperate because the pumps could only blow the air in one direction. To change direction or move the ball on an angle, you needed someone else's help.

Family Pastimes sells many games based on this principle, but you can make them as well. In a book of activities to help children learn self-control,

(*Jumpin' Jake Settles Down*, Shapiro, Childswork/Childsplay, LLC, 1993), I describe how to make a cooperative game where children use straws to blow a wad of paper around a simple maze (see next page). Like in every cooperative game, you can't help but learn to rely on others, and you can't help having fun. Other books on cooperative games include *New Games* and *New Games for the Whole Family* by Dale LeFevre (Putnam Publishing, 1988) and *Playfair* (Impact Publishing, 1980).

#76. Parent Support Groups

Theory: *Self-Help, Group Therapy*

It is sometimes difficult for people from other countries to understand the role that psychology plays in the American culture. No other country in history has been quite so fascinated with the psychological problems of individuals or so committed to helping them.

Perhaps it is that we are so mobile and that psychological values have taken the place of more traditional family and community values. Or perhaps it is our genetic inheritance as a nation of immigrants that causes us to search for answers and not accept the status quo. Whatever the reason, therapists and counselors can benefit from the societal drive for parents to want to understand themselves and their children.

Self-help groups designed for people in "recovery" have been a part of our culture for decades. But more recently, particularly in the past 10 years, there has been a tremendous interest in parents joining groups designed to help children with problems. There can be no question about the helpfulness of these groups. They provide important information to help parents understand their child's problem; they act as lobbying groups to obtain better educational and rehabilitative services for their children; and they act as a source of emotional support, providing a unique base of empathy and practical help for parents who might otherwise feel isolation and despair.

The most active of all parent support groups has been CHADD. (Children and Adults with Attention Deficit Disorder). Five years after its founding, this group has grown to more than 32,000 members with over 500 chapters

Here's a game that is much easier when you have someone else to help. You will need eight pencils, a cup, two straws, and a small wad of paper. Arrange the pencils in a double zigzag and place the cup at the end, as pictured below. Now wad up a three-inch square of paper. Score a goal by blowing the paper around the square and into the cup. Since the air you blow through the straw can only go in one direction, you will find it much easier when both players cooperate, blowing on the paper simultaneously.

See how fast you can complete the maze without going outside the lines.

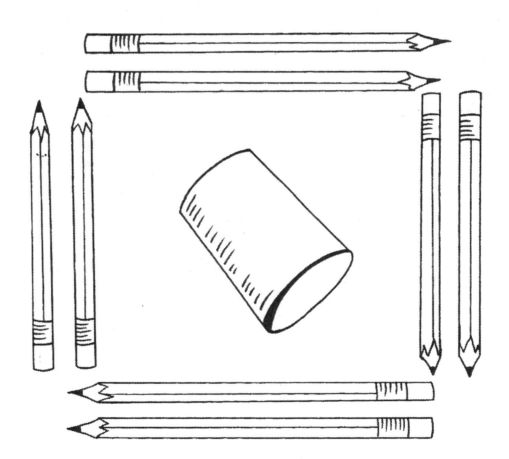

The Maze Game

around the country, and it has become a major factor in the increasing number of educational services and products for these children.

Connecting parents with an appropriate support group can be an invaluable psychological technique. Therapists and counselors should have a list of all relevant support associations in their areas and, if possible, should contact the heads of these local chapters to know when the chapters meet, their schedule of activities, their goals, and so on. The following is a partial listing of some of the national support groups:

American Association for Protecting Children
c/o American Humane Association
63 Inverness Drive East
Englewood, CO 80112-5117
(303) 792-9900

International Society for Prevention of Child Abuse and Neglect
200 North Michigan Avenue, Suite 500
Chicago, IL 60601
(312) 578-1401

National Foundation to Prevent Child Sexual Abuse
6218 Beachway Drive, Box 1776
Falls Church, VA 22041(703) 820-1040

Anxiety Disorders Association of America
11900 Parklawn Drive, Suite 100
Rockville, MD 20852
(301) 231-9350

Obsessive Compulsive Information Center
Madison Institute of Medicine
7617 Mineral Point Rd., Suite 300
Madison, WI 53717
(608) 827-2470

Children and Adults with Attention Deficit Disorder (CHADD)
8181 Professional Place, Suite 201
Landover, MD 20785
(800) 233-4050

Building a Strong Self-Concept

Self-esteem has long been recognized as an important issue to be addressed in any type of therapy or counseling. It is assumed that having low self-esteem contributes to a host of psychological problems and that having high self-esteem is the best way to prevent problems from occurring.

There are some people who think our national interest in helping children with their self-esteem is a misguided form of self-absorption, but they are confusing self-esteem with self-love. Having a good sense of self-esteem is much more than valuing and accepting oneself. That is just the beginning. True self-esteem must be viewed in a social context and defined in terms of the child's total personality development. Children with a good self-concept will see themselves as valuable people, whose sense of selfworth and belonging are reflected by their internal sense of success and mastery, as well as from the approval of their family, community, and society at large.

Building a Strong Self-Concept
by Teaching Responsibility
#77. Becoming More Independent
#78. Learning to Accept Responsibility

Theory: *Values Clarification*

It is my personal belief that the best way to help a child build a good self-concept is by helping him or her "be good." Research has suggested that children who are perceived as being good–considerate of others, responsible, well-mannered–receive more positive attention from both adults and peers. It is most important to teach these values in the day-to-day lives of the children, but therapists and counselors can also have a role focusing the parents and teachers on this important way to develop a child's self-concept.

The following exercises were taken from *The Building Blocks of Self-Esteem* (Shapiro, Childswork/Childsplay, LLC, 1993), a book I wrote to help therapists and teachers give "therapeutic homework" to build a child's self-concept along with regular academic assignments.

#79. Community-Based Interventions

Theory: *Reality Therapy, Activity Group Therapy, Systems Interventions*

Most therapists today confront considerably more than a child's intrapsychic problems. Many children who end up in therapy come from a less than-ideal home. Other children have the burden of coming from a disadvantaged background, living in substandard housing, being exposed to gangs and drugs on an almost daily basis, and having to cope with prejudice and cultural differences as well. For these children, individual therapy is clearly not enough.

Fortunately, there are hundreds of community-based programs around the country, and while they may not be called "therapy," they nevertheless have a therapeutic benefit for many children, providing a sense of belonging, self-confidence, security, and personal power. Most of these groups are activity-based, teaching members real-life skills that will help them become successful adults.

One of the more interesting success stories in community intervention originated with two teenagers in New Haven, Connecticut. Duke Porter and La'rie McGruder believed that teens communicate best with kids their own age, and after they were trained as community mediators they began a series of workshops called "Survivin' N Da Hood" based around a role-playing game. In the game, participants have to decide to go to one of three areas: a party, a job, or school. The party sounds good, but when you're there you are exposed to drug use, venereal disease and AIDS. Meanwhile, with every roll of the dice, the years are passing, and so maybe you think you'll go get a job. The game asks how much money you would like to make in a week. Five hundred dollars? You'll have to sell drugs. How else are you going to make that much money without an education? Decide it's time to get an education? A good choice, but now you're older, and you'll still have

Becoming More Independent

As kids grow up, they learn to do more and more things for themselves. They become more independent.

Some things kids learn to do aren't much fun, like picking up their clothes or doing hard chores. But there are many more things that kids really like doing as they become more independent, like sleeping at a friend's house, going shopping by themselves, and earning extra money by mowing the lawn or shoveling the snow for neighbors.

Tom, however, couldn't see the point of becoming independent. He would say, "My mother will do it anyway, so why should I bother?"

Take a good look at Tom in his room. Can you find five things he didn't do? (The answers are upside down at the bottom of this page).

What are the things that you like to do that show you are independent?

_____

_____

Answers: 1) tie his shoes 2) wash his face and hands 3) put his toys away 4) make his bed 5) practice his saxophone

116

Learning to Accept Responsibility

This family looks unhappy because everyone has lost something in this room. Can you find what each person has lost? Who do you think lost what? Can you find all 10 things that are lost? (Keys, doll, truck, glove, purse, sock, boots, books, pet rabbit and toy mouse).

to face many difficult decisions about supporting yourself, relationships with others, and so on.

Using the game as a springboard, the group has formed a "Survivin' N Da Hood" club that works with high school drop-outs and ex-gang members as well as straight "A" students. The goal of the group is to teach teens to make responsible choices and to spread this message through workshops and public speaking. The group also plans to provide summer and/or year-round employment for its members so that they can have an income rather than resort to selling drugs or other crimes.

To find out about similar groups in your community, you may have to do some research. Start with local recreation, mental health, and human service agencies. Don't forget church groups and charitable organizations, which often support such projects. Also, local newspapers are a great resource. They frequently profile these groups and can put you in touch with community leaders.

#80. Sports as Therapy

Theory: *Developmental*

Sports can be an important avenue for many children to develop a positive self-concept, and yet most therapists (recreational therapists are the notable exception) neglect to see the importance of athletics in a child's development. There is no doubt that we are an increasingly sedentary nation; more children than ever suffer from obesity and fall below age expectations on tests of physical strength and endurance. And yet exercise of almost any type makes us feel good at any age, and "feeling good" is one of the most important goals of psychotherapy. In addition, organized sports give children the important peer interaction and sense of belonging that sets the foundation for future social success.

Dr. Eric Margenau, Director of the Center for Sports Psychology in New York City, explains that sports, like books, music, and art, are among life's important growth experiences (*Sports without Pressure: A Guide for Parents and Coaches of Young Athletes*, Gardner Press, 1990). Dr. Margenau encourages parents to remember:

1. Sports are fun and should be kept fun.

2. Competition is fine, but it should be kept friendly, emphasizing participation rather than outcome.

3. Parents should not pressure a child to excel, regardless of ability.

When recommending participation in sports as a therapeutic technique, the therapist or counselor must try to manipulate the experience so that it is as positive as possible. It is paramount that the therapist and the parents be

---

Parents: *Use the following form to help you determine your child's strengths at sports. Choose a sport that most closely matches his or her abilities and interests by checking off the statements that describe your child. Don't be discouraged by your child's lack of enthusiasm in sports. It is a very important part of his or her development.*

—Prefers group sports
—Prefers individual sports
—Has good hand-eye coordination
—Enjoys running
—Is stronger than many peers
—Watches a particular sport on TV (Which one?)
—Has parents, older siblings, close friends, etc. who have an interest/ ability in a particular sport (Which one?)
—Enjoys competition
—Dislikes competition
—Has time to spend at practice
—Has friends who enjoy a particular sport (Which one?)
—Feels he/she would enjoy a particular sport (Which one?)

Which sport(s) fit(s) the statements that you have checked?

_____

---

aware that competitive sports can be very negative experiences for some children, and above all, care should be taken so that a child isn't exposed to a demanding and critical coach or a situation where he or she is likely to be ridiculed or rejected by his or her peers.

In recommending athletics as a therapeutic strategy, the therapist must weigh the many benefits of sports against possible problems. To do this, I recommend that the parents fill out the form on page 119 to help them decide on the best possible sport for their child.

Once several sports have been selected in which the child is likely to succeed, the parent must now weigh external factors including: the availability of the sport, expense associated with the sport, time requirements of the sport, and temperament of instructor or coach who will work with the child.

#81. Special Time

Theory: *Client-Centered Therapy*

Children in therapy often receive disproportionately high amounts of criticism and other negative feedback. As a result, even if their behaviors improve and their problems recede, they may be left with a poor self-image, a sense of not being good enough.

Providing children with Special Time is a way to not only build a positive self-image but to give them the important benefits of having the unconditional attention and acceptance of which many children are deprived. Special Time is defined as a specific time during the day when the parent and the child can be alone together, and the parent agrees that he or she will not issue any corrective, critical or disparaging remarks. During this time (about 15 to 20 minutes is recommended), the child can choose any activity to engage in that does not require an expenditure of money, and of course, is safe.

This technique is extremely simple and rewarding. In fact, research suggests that when parents are given multiple techniques to help them deal with difficult children, Special Time is the technique that is most likely to be continued after therapy has terminated. This is not to say, however, that Special Time can be introduced to parents in an off-handed manner.

This technique, which is based on Rogerian or Client-Centered Therapy, requires the parent to actively ignore behaviors that might otherwise annoy them, to participate in an activity with children that might otherwise not interest them, and show their interest in the child by seeing the world through his eyes. For some parents, this is not an easy thing to do. The parent may wish to control the situation or become distracted. Usually practicing this intervention with the therapist present is the best way to teach the parent to understand the significance of taking a nondirective, nonjudgmental stance.

Play Techniques

In this final section, I will discuss a variety of play techniques that can be used to help the therapist or counselor focus on different problems. For the most part, they are adaptable to a wide variety of therapeutic situations and problems.

Naturalistic Therapeutic Games
#82. Self-Esteem Musical Chairs
#83. "I Can Do It" Arm Wrestling
#84. Therapeutic Games for Car Rides

Theory: *Developmental; Cognitive Behavior Modification*

Games have always fascinated me as a psychological technique for their versatility in eliciting a virtually unlimited number of therapeutic experiences. Most therapists are familiar with published therapeutic board games but may not realize that there are many therapeutic games they can use with equally powerful effects that spring forth right from their own minds. I call these games "naturalistic games," because they are derivations of games that seem to be a natural part of childhood play, many of which are passed on from generation to generation. These games have all the playful elements of the original game but vary slightly to serve a therapeutic purpose.

Self-Esteem Musical Chairs is an adaptation of a familiar childhood game played with children between the ages of 4 and 8. In the original version, you start with a group of children who must circle a line of chairs while the music plays. When the music stops, all the children must grab a chair, except that there is one chair less than the number of children, and so one child in each round is left out and cannot play for the remainder of the game.

Naturally, when children are left out they feel somewhat badly, particularly if this happens all the time. But children never feel badly when they play Self-Esteem Musical Chairs. In this version of the game, when a child is "out" because he or she couldn't find a chair, the group recognizes that this is not a pleasant experience even though it is part of the game. Each time a player is out, all the other players must say something nice about that player, for example: "You're a good sport." "I like the shirt you have on." "You are the fastest runner in the class." This exercise forces young children to see the positive attributes of all the members of the group and changes the focus of the game from winning or losing to reinforcing each other's self-worth.

"I Can Do It" Arm Wrestling is not so much a technique in itself as it is a demonstration of the spontaneous ways that naturalistic games can be used. I have only played this game once, with Sam, a learning-disabled eleven-year-old boy and his six-year-old brother, Chris. Through most of the therapy, I saw Sam by himself, addressing his mild depression, lack of motivation in school, and occasional angry outbursts. His mother had told me that his relationship with his younger brother was worsening, however, and I suggested that I see both boys together for a few sessions.

It was not difficult to see why Sam disliked and picked on his younger brother; Chris seemed to have everything that Sam wanted. Chris was wiry and cute, while Sam was chubby and his classmates teased him about his appearance. Chris got straight A's in school, but Sam had trouble in every subject. Moreover, because of Chris's precociousness and Sam's apparent slowness, their parents treated them as equals in spite of their five-year age difference. They had the same bedtime, the same allowance, the same responsibilities and privileges.

Naturally, I counseled the parents to slowly begin to treat the boys differently. Sam was older and should be treated that way. But I also wanted to demonstrate to the boys that Sam, as the older brother, was not equal to but above his brother in the family hierarchy. To demonstrate Sam's "power" over his younger brother, I had the boys play a game of "I Can Do It" Arm Wrestling. The game was played like any other form of arm wrestling, except that when the winner forced the other person's arm to the table, he would say something special that he could do: "I can cook breakfast for the family," "I can do my multiplication tables," and so on.

Of course, there was one other therapeutic trick involved in this game: I knew that Sam would always win. He was over 50 pounds heavier than his brother, and he could easily beat Chris in arm wrestling, or any other kind of wrestling for that matter.

The boys played several times in my office, while I observed. I watched Chris's reaction even more closely than Sam's, waiting for him to proclaim this game "unfair," and yet he never said a word. With every round he lost, he smiled, listened to his brother's self-congratulatory statement, and then played again. I asked the boys to play at least two times at home before they came to the next session.

At the next session, I was surprised to hear that Sam and Chris had played the arm wrestling game every day. Most of the time, Chris had actually initiated the game, in spite of the fact that he continued to lose all the time. It appeared that Chris liked losing to his older brother. Although at first I was surprised by Chris's reaction, I remembered that when a successful strategic intervention is made in the family, the family members are frequently relieved to be placed in a developmentally more appropriate role. Sam and Chris occasionally played this game on their own through the remainder of their time in therapy. For all I know, they are still playing it today.

The idea of encouraging parents to play Therapeutic Car Games came to me after a mother was complaining about how her two children fought and nagged her on their daily one-half hour commute to their suburban private school. My first response was to simply suggest that they each have a bag of small toys or other things to do during the commute, but then it occurred to me: Why not use this time to work on therapeutic goals?

The mother was seeing me because her children were having an adverse reaction to her recent separation. There had been a good deal of acrimony between the parents, and the boy and girl had both become very moody—sometimes sullen and withdrawn and at other times angry and defiant. Both children denied that their parents" divorce had anything to do with their behavior.

It occurred to me that the car ride would be an excellent opportunity for the children to talk with their mother and that a game would be the way to make this happen. I asked the mother to instruct her children on playing a

Feelings License Plate Game. You play by finding license plates that had two letters of a "feelings" word. In other words:

AS4 532   Sad

PR 314   Proud

AMT 222   Mad

Once you spot a plate with at least two letters of a feelings word, in any order, you then have to say something that makes you feel that way.

The children, at ages eight and ten, were smart enough to see through the purpose of this game (and after all, "the shrink" had suggested it), and yet with the added motivation of winning a chip each time they spotted a feelings license plate, they readily agreed to play. The chips were totaled and collected at the end of the week, and the winner got to choose an activity that the family would do together on the weekend.

Therapeutic Game You Can Make
#85. Anything I Want Checkers
#86. "Pass the Egg" Game
#87. The Make-a-Game Technique

Theory: *Client-Centered Therapy; Strategic Family Therapy; Cognitive Behavior Modification*

A slightly more sophisticated category of games that can be used in therapy are what I refer to as "therapist-made games." These go beyond naturalistic games in that they involve making a physical game with readily available and inexpensive parts. These games are not really different from many of the published therapeutic games that are available, with the exception that the therapist or counselor does the work of actually making the physical game. In spite of its many merits, however, I still find that this technique meets with considerable resistance from therapists.

As a group, therapists and counselors don't like to make things. They go into the profession primarily attracted by the intellectual challenge and the opportunity to use their verbal skills to better the lives of others.

Unless they become art therapists, the vast majority of people who work with children are not interested in cutting, pasting, drawing, and the like, even though the end result may be a powerful therapeutic tool. However, if you can get past this small prejudice, and you can tolerate a few visits to the stationery or art store, you will find an inexpensive and fascinating way to do therapy to which children readily respond.

Anything I Want Checkers is not really what I call this technique when presenting it to children, but rather the name I give it when explaining the game to other therapists. What I mean by the name is that with an inexpensive set of checkers, along with a few stationery items, I can get the child to respond to almost any subject that I want. I can have the child talk about family problems, feelings about classmates, fears and worries, etc. When the rules of the game say that you should respond to a card, most children will readily do so.

The game is as simple as it is versatile. Just randomly place different colored dots obtained at any stationery store (up to four different colors) on all the checkers. Then get correspondingly colored index cards, and on each set of cards, write down questions to which you want the child to respond. For example:

Red Cards: Home

"What is thing you like to do best when you get home from school?"

"Who in your family gives you the most hugs?"

Blue Cards: Problems

"What is the worst problem you think kids have?"

"What would you do if you couldn't solve a problem by yourself?

Then, simply play checkers with one added rule: Every time you jump another player, you must pick up and respond to a card from the correspondingly colored deck. To prepare the game, you should write about 25 cards to go with each deck. If you like, have the child and/or the parents write cards as well.

Pass the Egg is a game I have used in getting resistant families to discuss their problems. The game requires the therapist to provide plastic eggs that come apart and can be opened, a radio or tape recorder, and a paper and pencil. Plastic eggs are readily available at Easter time, but if you can't find them, you can use any small container that can be opened to place something inside such as a small jewelry box (then, of course, the name of the game becomes "Pass the Box").

To begin, give each family member a piece of paper and a plastic egg. Instruct them to "Write a problem that families often have," and put it in the egg. Then put all the eggs, each containing a note from one family member, into a large bag.

Next the therapist should reach into the bag and pull out an egg. The therapist then tells the family that this game is played like "hot potato": People must pass the egg around while the music plays, and when it stops, the person holding the egg must open it, then read and answer the question.

Naturally, the therapist is in charge of the music and must turn away while the music is playing to make the game fair. The game is over when all the eggs have been picked and all the questions have been discussed.

This technique can also be used with a group of children who have something in common. The directions would change to something like: "Write an idea about how kids can get along better in your class" or "Write down a problem that children whose parents are divorced frequently have." Then the person who gets the egg must discuss the statement inside.

The Make-a-Game Technique (see *Short-Term Therapy with Children*, Shapiro, Childswork/Childsplay, LLC, 1994) refers to a two-step process in which the therapist makes a board game designed for the unique needs of a patient and then plays it with the patient or the patient's family. Although there are nearly 100 therapeutic board games that have been published, there is no game that is as effective as the one you make for an individual child.

The first step in the process is the actual making of the game. This generally takes two to three sessions and gives the therapist a rare opportunity to create something for and with a child. In making the game, I suggest using a prototype board, such as those on the next two pages.

Game-making kits are also available from Creative Education of Canada (704 Mara St., Point Edward, ON, N7V1X4; (519) 337-5685). In designing the game, the therapist first has to decide on the therapeutic intent. Is it designed to help the child reflect on his problems? Is it designed to bring two family members together? Will it teach the child about divorce, or how to handle loss, or stress-reduction techniques? In general, therapeutic games can do five different things: provide diagnostic information, teach children about a specific theme, teach the child a cognitive or behavioral skill, help children communicate, and teach children cooperation.

The two most critical elements of the game will be the rules and the cards. The rules are the driving force behind every game. In psychodynamic terms, they represent the "reality principle." The rules must be written clearly and simply, and should address not only the psychological purpose of the game but also make the game fun (unless it is fun, it isn't a game). The rules and the cards are best written with the child. In constructing the game together, the therapist builds a relationship with the child by working towards a common goal.

129

130

Then the game has to be named. The name should always be stated in positive terms, for example:

- The How-to-Get-Your-Homework-Done-on-Time Game

- The Finding Friends Game

- David's Game about Himself

The second step in this technique is, of course, the playing of the game. Often children like to make games to be played with a person other than the therapist. They may want to show off a little and also to communicate on a conscious or unconscious level with an important person in their life. The therapist should consider who will play the game from its inception, considering with the child who might be most appropriate.

Most of the time, the therapist will have to finish the game him- or herself before it is played. Children often get bored with the making of the game after two sessions, and yet it is rarely completely finished in this amount of time. The therapist should then get the child's permission to finish the game (particularly in writing the cards and rules) for a test-play during the next session.

#88. Stories That Teach Reality

Theory: *Bibliotherapy*

In the last 10 years, there has been a tremendous interest in psychologically oriented books for children, and, as a result, bibliotherapy has become one of the most popular of all therapeutic techniques. There are many types of books written for children, such as books that present the child with role models or books that give the child information about a particular problem that they may be having, but there is none quite so intriguing as the therapeutic fable or fairy tale. In these books, instead of things happening to people because of magic or witchcraft, the heroes take responsibility for their lives: Cinderella doesn't wait for her Prince Charming but decides to join a dating service. The Ugly Duckling does not just turn into a swan but finds value in things about himself other than his appearance. Two popular collections of these stories by Dr. Richard A. Gardner are *Fairy Tales for Today's Children* and *Modern Fairy Tales* (published by Creative Therapeutics, Cresskill, NJ).

Reading these stories with children can be an effective therapeutic technique in itself, but helping children rewrite their own favorite fairy tales can be even more meaningful.

Start by having the child tell you a fairy tale or fable as he or she knows it, and write it down verbatim, only filling in parts that the child asks you to help with. Write it like a book, with each new idea on a separate page. Write the story as the child tells it on the top half of the pages only. Leave the bottom half of the pages blank.

Once the story has been written, take some time to talk about the story, finding out what the child thinks about it. Most popular fables or fairy tales are about problems that the protagonist encounters and then are solved by magic or good fortune, rather than through realistic thinking, problem-solving, and good decision-making. On the bottom half of each page of the original fairy tale, ask the child to help you write a new, modern version of the story, emphasizing the coping skills and problem-solving ability of the protagonist.

It is okay for the therapist to fill in ideas to help the child. The idea is to encourage problem-solving or realistic thinking that the child can apply to other areas of his or her life.

Let's say the child has chosen the story of Goldilocks and the Three Bears. Here is a way that the story could be rewritten:

Once upon a time there was a girl named Goldilocks.
Once upon a time there was a girl named Sara Gold.

She lived near the forest with her grandma.
She lived in the city, on the edge of a big park.

One day she was walking in the forest by herself.
*Sara knew better than to walk alone in the park, so she
asked her best friend Harry to go along.*

She came upon a small house, deep in the forest.

> *Sara and Harry came across a small house, but weren't sure that they should go into the house. It could have been private property or it could have been part of the park. Was it dangerous?*

When the story has been completed, the child can go back and illustrate the modern version of the story.

Uses of Videotape
#89. Videos of Therapy as Homework
#90. Videos in Parent Training
#91. The Video Self-Modeling Technique

Theory: *Behavior Modification; Learning Theory*

In my opinion, videotape is one of the most underutilized techniques in treating children. The video camera not only records information that the therapist could never see but plays it back for a variety of purposes.

In a recent interview with Dr. Richard A. Gardner (*Conduct Disorders of Childhood*, Childswork/Childsplay, 1994), he explained how he videotapes all of his therapy sessions, making two copies, one of which he often sends home with the parents to watch as "therapeutic homework." When asked about the issue of confidentiality, Gardner explained that for children between the ages four and ten, confidentiality is usually a nonissue.

He explains that in the vast majority of cases, children expect that the parents will be kept informed of what is happening in the therapy (with an exception, of course, when the child is in therapy for abuse or mistreatment by the parent). After all, the parent already knows that the child is soiling, or lying, or stealing, since he or she is the one who brought the child there!

Unlike Dr. Gardner, most therapists prefer to edit the videos that they show as part of their parent training. I use a video camera as a way to train parents and teachers in the use of therapeutic games. Therapeutic games are one of the best techniques to extend therapy outside the office. But simply handing the game to a parent or teacher is rarely enough.

Instead, I will videotape myself playing the game with the child and then show the parent or teacher (whom I treat as a cotherapist) a few segments of the tape.

While videotaping the game, I will point out ways that I respond to encourage or motivate the child towards the therapeutic goal. In other circumstances, I may ask the parents to videotape themselves playing the game with the child at home. Then I will review the tape with them, again training them as cotherapists.

The Video-Therapy Self-Modeling Technique created by Michael Greelis and Betsy Harmann (*The ABCs of Video-Therapy*, Academic Therapy Publications, 1980) takes video editing to a more sophisticated level, blending video technology with basic principles of behavior modification. The technique is based on one of the classic studies in behavioral psychology by R. Bandura, who demonstrated that children left alone in a room will imitate the aggressive actions of other children that they see in a movie or on a video monitor. The basic format of the Video-Therapy Self-Modeling Technique assumes that if children will imitate the negative things that they see on TV, then they may also imitate positive ones. The technique goes on to assume that the child will be even more open to the positive videotape if he sees himself in the video, doing a new positive task. Tasks can include new social skills, assertive behavior, self-control techniques, and so on.

To make the self-modeling video, the therapist has the child practice the new behavior and then records it on videotape. The therapist then edits the tape so that it shows five or ten minutes of the child performing the task perfectly. Video editing can easily be done with just a video camera and a second recorder. Instructions for video editing come with most cameras. In addition, the therapist can dub in comments and "praise" on the video. Video titles can be easily added by videotaping homemade signs.

When the videotape is done, the child is instructed to watch it at least 10 times, preferably on 10 successive days. Children should be encouraged to invite parents or other relatives to watch the tape as well, as it is something to be proud of. The theory behind this technique is that the child will get a positive image of him- or herself doing the new behavior, making it more likely that the behavior will be accomplished in real-life situations.

#92. Using Dreams to Help Children: The Dream Journal

Theory: *Psychodynamic; Jungian Psychotherapy; Humanistic Psychotherapy*

Dreams have often been called "the gateway to the unconscious," and dream interpretation has been an important part of adult psychotherapy as practiced by psychoanalytic or Jungian therapists. But "dream work" may also have a place in child psychotherapy, particularly with children who have deep-seated emotional conflicts.

Those of us who work with children and tend to be more behaviorally-oriented may be put off by the "magic and mysticism" associated with dream interpretation. But *Dreams Can Help*, a dream workbook for children by Jonni Kincher (Free Spirit Publishing, 1988), takes a very practical, downto-earth look at dreams, making it a very accessible approach for many child therapists. The book begins matter-of-factly, with a review of the facts that we know about dreaming. For example: the average person has more than 1,000 dreams per year; almost all animals dream; bottlenose dolphins can sleep and be awake at the same time because they have the ability to use one side of their brain at a time and can literally have one side of their brain active while the other is asleep!

Then the author suggests how keeping a dream journal might stimulate creativity and insight into one's problems. The author cautions children that they are the only ones who can really know what a dream "means" to them; no one else can interpret a dream for them.

Can children really interpret their own dreams, or are dreams too abstract for young children to understand? Read this interpretation by an eight-year-old and decide for yourself:

> My parents leave me and my two brothers at the movies while they go across the street to shop at the K-Mart. The movie is about Dracula. Dracula comes out of the movie screen and tries to get us. We run. I run up the stairs by the side of the screen. I am running up the stairs and suddenly Dracula is not chasing

me – he is at the top of the stairs! Then my parents pick us all up.

WHAT I THINK MY DREAM MEANS: When I run from something, it will just be waiting for me at the top of the stairs.

(from *Dreams Can Help* by Jonni Kincher, p. 51)

#93. Solving Nightmares with Doll Play

Theory: *Psychodynamic Psychotherapy*

Young children frequently complain of recurring nightmares which can be associated with a difficult life event, such as a divorce. Or nightmares can seemingly appear out of nowhere, surprising adults with their intensity and terror. One technique that has proven to be successful with children who have "bad" dreams is to have them act out the nightmare and add a "resolution" to the dream with dolls. The therapist will need a variety of small figures, a doll house, and other props. If the child's dreams include elements that the therapist doesn't have in his or her playroom (tunnels, witches, etc.), photographs or drawings will do.

The parent is asked to write down the dream as soon as the child can recount it. Some children will remember their dreams well enough to tell them to the therapist without having them written down immediately, but most will only remember the effect associated with the dream or a few of the dream elements. In the session, the therapist will read the dream and ask the child to act out the dream with the small figures and props. If the child is reluctant to do this, the therapist can act out the scene him- or herself.

Once the dream is acted out as it was originally recorded, the therapist asks the child if he or she can think of a better way for it to end, asking him or her to act out a better resolution of the dream. Instead of being chased by monsters, the child can have the monsters destroyed by a jet plane, with him- or herself as the pilot. Instead of being lost in a scary forest, the child can bring a compass and find his or her way to a telephone and call home.

With each resolution, the therapist can guide the child towards bringing about a more appropriate ending to the dream, with the child as the central character who brings about the positive change.

Some children, particularly young children, are too wary of their bad dreams to talk about them or play them out. But this technique can be just as effective if the therapist plays out the scenes, again emphasizing the child as the central actor. The message of this technique will always be the same, "Dreams are not real. They are things we make up in our mind. We can make up answers to our dreams while we are awake, too! We can learn ways to conquer our fears."

Using Concrete Imagery to Teach Self-Control
#94. The Turtle Technique to Control Aggression
#95. Blowing Imaginary Bubbles to Relax

Theory: *Behavior Modification*

Young children are highly suggestible when you work them through the language of metaphoric play. When you give children a play assignment to help them learn a new behavior, they are much more likely to use it than when you simply ask them directly to stop a particular behavior.

The Turtle Technique was originally designed for use in the classroom to help young children control their anger. (Robin, Schneider, and Dolnick. "The Turtle Technique: An Extended Case Study of Self-Control in the Classroom." *Psychology in the Schools*, 13: 449-453). When children are upset, they are told to think of a turtle withdrawing into its shell, pulling its arms and legs tightly to its body, closing its eyes, and lowering its head. When in this position, the child cannot be aggressive. In effect, this technique teaches a new behavioral response to situations that would normally lead to aggression.

The technique is introduced with a story about a little turtle who gets into trouble frequently. One day, a very old, wise turtle shows the little turtle how to use protection and withdraw into his shell. The wise turtle tells the little turtle to stay there and relax until he feels calmer, then think things through. The little turtle tries and no longer gets into trouble.

The child is taught a four-step process to using the turtle response as a substitute for aggression:

1. Identify specific situations or cues that normally result in an aggressive response, such as when a child is being teased by another child or when a child feels frustrated and in danger of losing control.

2. Practice using the Turtle Technique in role-play situations. Have children participate in an activity and when the adult

says "turtle," the children must immediately get into the "turtle" posture. This could be played as a game, a type of "freeze tag."

3. The child should practice responding to a turtle "sign" by the adult (an open hand that is closed in a fist). The teacher, for example, could use this sign to cue the child to gain self-control on the playground or at other times when the child is likely to be aggressive.

4. Finally, the child should be expected to cue him- or herself and use the Turtle Technique in appropriate circumstances. He or she should be able to report instances when he or she has used the turtle technique without any external cue.

Another self-control technique used to teach a child deep-breathing is the Bubble Technique. Rather than just instructing the child to breathe deeply in and out, the therapist instructs the child to imagine that he or she is using a very special bubble pipe. He or she should imagine him- or herself taking a big breath and then slowly, slowly, letting the air out so that the bubble can get as big as possible. This can actually be practiced using a real bubble pipe or bubble gum.

#96. The Life Space Interview

Theory: *Client-Centered Therapy*

Often, counselors and therapists are called upon to deal with children who are exhibiting distressing acting-out behaviors or emotional outbursts. When children are upset and their adrenaline is flowing, adults often feel helpless in the face of this intense reaction. Adults are likely to respond much more positively when they have rehearsed a set procedure for dealing with these difficult situations.

One such procedure is the Life Space Interview, originally developed by Fritz Redl and elaborated by Wood and Long (*Life Space Intervention: Talking With Children and Youth in Crisis*, 1990). The technique has two parts, one reactive and one proactive. When the child is in crisis, the adult should carry out five general principles:

1. Help the child verbalize feelings rather than act them out.

2. Help the child manage feelings of panic, fury, and guilt by remaining calm and talking about alternative ways to address the immediate problem.

3. Maintain communication by talking about things that are nonthreatening to the child.

4. Remind the child of the rules and the consequences for breaking them.

5. Help the child recognize the choices that he or she can make and their pluses and minuses.

After the episode, the adult should take the time to consider the issues that led to the original outburst:

1. Reality check: clear up distortions or irrational ideas that may have led to the outburst.

2. Confront secondary gains. Consider what the child is achieving by his or her acting-out (e.g., getting attention) and find more acceptable ways for the child to meet these needs.

3. Address issues around the child's underlying values and needs.

4. Teach the child alternative reactions to stressful events and practice them.

The most important thing that therapists can do for adults working with difficult children is to give them a systematic strategy for helping these children and rehearsing it with them until it becomes second nature.

#97. The Color-Your-Life Technique

Theory: *Psychodynamic*

Dr. Kevin O'Connor describes The Color-Your-Life Technique as a method of increasing children's awareness of affective states, and encouraging the discussion of events on an affective level, a way to transition the child from action-oriented play to verbalization, and as a way to assess a child's past and present affective states (The Color-Your-Life Technique by Kevin O'Connor, in *The Handbook of Play Therapy*, Schaefer and O'Connor, eds., John Wiley and Sons, 1983). The technique begins by having the child pair different emotional states with different colors. Typically the child will associate common affective states with specific colors: Red/Anger, Yellow/Happiness, Blue/Sadness, Green/Jealousy. But the child may have other reasons to pair colors with different feelings as well. Dr. O'Connor recommends limiting the number of pairs to eight or nine.

Once the color-feeling pairs are established, the child is given a piece of blank paper and told to "fill the paper with colors that show all the feelings that you have had in your life." Some further explanation is usually needed as well.

> If you have been happy about half the time in your life, then half the paper should be yellow. If you have been happy your whole life, with no other feelings, then you should color the whole paper yellow.

> (O'Connor, p. 253, *The Handbook of Play Therapy*)

The child is told that he or she can use the colors any way that he or she wants adding squares, circles, designs, and so on. During the coloring, the child is encouraged to discuss feelings about specific life events. The technique can be used in individual or group psychotherapy and works best with children ages six to twelve.

Using Art Techniques in Groups
#98. The Collaborative Drawing Technique
#99. The Use of Clay in Self -Control Groups

Theory: *Family Systems Therapy; Behavior Modification*

Another interesting use of art techniques, The Collaborative Drawing Technique, was introduced in the early 1980s by Gavin Smith ("The Collaborative Drawing Technique," *Journal of Personality Assessment*, 49:582-585). This technique was designed for use in family or couples' therapy and combines the use of projective art interpretation with the excitement and challenge of a game.

The technique is introduced as a nonverbal task to the family. It requires only a few simple materials: a selection of crayons, a large sheet of paper (at least 11" X 17"), a stopwatch, a chair and a desk. The participants are told to select one crayon each, and that they will be drawing family pictures, with one person at a time doing the drawing.

During the first "round," each person works on the picture for 30 seconds. Then the next person draws. The therapist monitors the drawing, and when 30 seconds are up, the next person gets in the drawing chair and begins. During subsequent rounds, the time limit is progressively reduced to 25, 20, 15, 10, 5, and, finally, 3 seconds. Smith notes that this continual reduction of the drawing time heightens the gamelike atmosphere, reduces resistance, and decreases the chance of intellectualizing the task.

During the drawing, the therapist discourages questions and discussion. However, when the task is completed, the therapist asks pointed questions about the family dynamics that were revealed in the game, such as who cheated, who used the most space on the paper and who the least, where are the places on the drawing where two people worked together, what is your reaction to the final product, and what parts of the exercise reminded you of the way the family works together?

Clay is a more primitive art medium that seems particularly relevant to groups of young children working on self-control. Various exercises have been designed for working with groups of children to help them express their feelings in a controlled manner as well as to practice self-control. Here are a few:

1. One at a time, pound the clay as flat as you can. Each time you hit the clay, say something that makes you angry.

2. Roll the clay into a "snake." When I say "go," each person should stretch the snake as slowly as he or she can. The last person to break his or her snake is the winner.

3. Start with a ball of clay and pass it around the table. Each

person has 60 seconds to shape the ball of clay into a com mon object. The other members of the group must guess what that object is.

4. Start with a large ball of clay. The group has three minutes to make a large string of clay to form a circle that connects all the group members. Group members must not speak with or touch each other, and each person must work with his or her nondominant hand. If anyone speaks, leaves his or her seat or touches another person, the group has to start all over again.

Helping People Find Their Own Solutions
#100. The Search for Solutions
#101. Communicating Solutions

Theory: *Solution-Oriented Brief Therapy*

Dr. Steve de Shazer (*Keys to Solutions in Brief Therapy*, W.W. Norton and Co., 1985) suggests that one of the most important ways therapists can work with people is to help them see their own solutions. He suggests that in the vast majority of cases, people already know the solutions to their problems, but these solutions are inaccessible to them. Dr. de Shazer uses the metaphor of knowing that you have something but that it is behind a locked door. The therapy provides a key to this locked door. But while these locks may be very complicated, de Shazer explains, the keys that fit these locks can be fairly simple. The therapist can use "skeleton keys" that fit many locks, helping the patients to find the right keys to unlock the doors to their solutions.

While Solution-Oriented Therapy was predominantly designed for use with adults, the principles can also be applied to work with parents and teachers. Parents often come to the therapist or the counselor in a "state of ignorance." They are at a complete loss as to what to do with their child. But how can that be? In the vast majority of cases, they are competent people who solve problems every day. They find and hold jobs, manage their budgets, fix things when they are broken ... they solve complex problems all the time. It is the therapist's job, then, to reinforce their competency and problem-solving skills. The therapist can "empower" the parents by focusing them on their successes rather than on their sense of failure. This is best done by helping them see an analogy relating the current problem they are having with their child to a problem they have solved in the past.

Dr. William Hudson O'Hanlon of the Hudson Center for Brief Therapy in Omaha, Nebraska, also advocates the Solution-Oriented Approach, stressing the need for communicating to patients that they can find their own solutions. O'Hanlon suggests many communication strategies to help people focus on solutions, including:

- Creating an expectation for change with solution-oriented language.

- Identifying the first signs that indicate movement towards a goal.

- Paying attention to small changes.

- Suggesting changes in the way the problem is viewed.

- Reminding people of past solutions to problems.

- Listening for connecting themes that allow people to relate one solution to another.

Communicating solutions is equally important when working with teachers or other professionals in a school or institutional setting. There is a natural tendency among groups of professionals to speak informally in the hallway or lunchroom, and even the best-intentioned therapists and counselors can be drawn into conversations that are "gossipy" or parody the child's problem. This type of communication is perfectly understandable; it allows professionals to let off steam and form a bond. But unfortunately it doesn't help the child. Like it or not, every time you say a word as a mental health professional you are having an effect on the child and the way people view and treat that child. You can use every contact with a teacher or other helping professional to aid them in seeing solutions. This may not make you the most popular person in your school or agency; you'll know this when people start ducking into their rooms and offices as you walk down the hall. But go after them. Chase them down. A word or moment that helps a child is never regretted.

INDEX

REFERENCES

Azrin, Nathan and Nunn, Gregory. *Habit Control in a Day.* New York: Pocket Books, 1977.

Baille, Martin. *Magic Fun.* New York: Little, Brown and Co., 1992.

Barkley, Russell. *Attention Deficit Hyperactivity Disorder.* New York: Guilford Publications, 1990.

Beck, Aaron. *The Cognitive Theory of Depression.* New York: Guilford, 1979.

Conari Press Editors. *Kids' Random Acts of Kindness.* Berkeley: Conari Press, 1994.

Conari Press Editors. *Random Acts of Kindness.* Berkley: Conari Press, 1994.

De Shazer, Steve. *Keys to Solutions in Brief Therapy.* New York: W.W. Norton, Inc., 1985.

Faber, Adele, and Mazlish, Elaine. *How to Talk So Kids Will Listen and Listen So Kids Will Talk.* New York: Avon Books, 1980.

Gardner, Richard A. *Fairy Tales for Today's Children.* Cresskill: Creative Therapeutics, 1982.

Gardner, Richard A. *Modern Fairy Tales.* Cresskill: Creative Therapeutics, 1984.

Gardner, Richard A. *Pick-and-Tell Games.* Cresskill: Creative Therapeutics, 1984.

Gardner, Richard A. *Psychotherapeutic Approaches with the Resistant Child.* New York: Jason Aaronson, 1975.

Gardner, Richard A. *The Psychotherapeutic Techniques of Richard A. Gardener, M.D.* Cresskill: Creative Therapeutics, 1992.

Gauchman, Wong, and Shapiro. *The A.D.D Tool Kit.* Plainview: Childswork/Childsplay, 1994.

Goldstein, Sam and Michael. *Managing Attention Disorders in Children.* New York: John Wiley and Sons, Inc., 1990.

Goldstein, Sam and Michael. New York: John Wiley and Sons, Inc., 1990.

Greelis, Michael and Harmann, Betsey. *The ABCs of Video-Therapy.* Novato: Academic Therapy Publications, 1980.

Hart, Archibald W. *Stress and Your Child.* New York: Word Publishers, 1992.

Kincher, Jonni. *Dreams Can Help.* Minneapolis: Free Spirit Publishing, 1988.

LeFevre, Dale. *New Games.* New York: Putnam Publishing, 1988.

LeFevre, Dale. *New Games for the Whole Family.* New York: Putnam Publishing, 1988.

Lewis, Barbara A. *The Kid's Guide to Social Action.* Minneapolis: Free Spirit Publishing, 1991.

March, John. *How I Ran OCD Off My Land: A Guide to the Cognitive Behavioral Treatment of Obsessive Compulsive Disorders in Children.* Durham: Self-Published, 1995.

Margenau, Eric. *Sports Without Pressure: A Guide for Parents and Coaches of Young Athletes.* New York: Gardner Press, 1990.

Nowicki, Steven, Jr., and Marshall, Duke. *Helping the Child Who Doesn't Fit In.* Atlanta: Peachtree Publishers, 1992.

O'Connor, Kevin. "The Color-Your-Life Technique," in *The Handbook of Play Therapy,* (Schaefer and O'Connor Editors). New York: John Wiley and Sons, 1983.

Party Magician Kit. The Watermill Press, 1993.

Robin Schneider and Dolnick. "The Turtle Technique: An Extended Case Study of Self-Control in the Classroom," in *Psychology in the Schools,* 13: 449-453.

Shapiro, Lawrence. *The Building Blocks of Self-Esteem.* Plainview: Childswork/Childsplay, 1993.

Shapiro, Lawrence. *Interviews with Experts in Child Psychotherapy.* Plainview: Childswork/Childsplay, 1994.

Shapiro, Lawrence. *Jumpin' Jake Settles Down.* Plainview: Childswork/Childsplay, 1994.

Shapiro, Lawrence. *Short-Term Therapy with Children.* Plainview: Childswork/Childsplay, LLC, 1994.

Smith, Gavin. "The Collaborative Drawing Technique," in *Journal of Personality Assessment,* 49: 582-585.

Tonge, B.J. *The International Book of Family Therapy*. New York: Brunner/Mazel, 1982.

Webster-Doyle, Terrence. *The Eye of the Hurricane*. Middlebury: Atrium Society, 1992.

Weinstein, Matt and Goodman, Joel. *Playfair*. Plantation: Impact Publishing, 1980.

Whitman, Cynthia. *Win the Whining War and Other Skirmishes: A Family Peace Plan.* Perspective Publishing, 1991.

Wood and Long. *Life Space Intervention: Talking with Children and Youth in Crisis,* 1990.

Ziegler, Robert, G. *Homemade Books to Help Kids Cope*. New York: Brunner/Mazel, 1993.